The MiG-29

RUSSIA'S LEGENDARY AIR SUPERIORITY, AND MULTIROLE FIGHTER,
1977 TO THE PRESENT

Andy Gröning

Schiffer Publishing Ltd

4880 Lower Valley Road • Atglen, PA 19310

Other Schiffer Books on Related Subjects:
MiG-29 Flight Manual by Alan R. Wise (978-0-7643-1389-9)
MiG Pilot Survival: Russian Aircrew Survival Equipment and Instruction by Alan R. Wise (978-0-7643-0130-8)
A Guide to the Russian Federation Air Force Museum at Monino by B. Korolkov & V. Kazashvili (978-0-7643-0076-9)

Originally published as MiG-29 by Motorbuch Verlag, Stuttgart, Germany © 2015.
www.paul-pietsch-verlage.de
Translated from the German by David Johnston

Cover design by Justin Watkinson
Type set in Corporate S/Corporate A

ISBN: 978-0-7643-5521-9
Printed in China

Published by Schiffer Publishing, Ltd.
4880 Lower Valley Road
Atglen, PA 19310
Phone: (610) 593-1777; Fax: (610) 593-2002
E-mail: Info@schifferbooks.com
Web: www.schifferbooks.com

For our complete selection of fine books on this and related subjects, please visit our website at www.schifferbooks.com. You may also write for a free catalog.

Schiffer Publishing's titles are available at special discounts for bulk purchases for sales promotions or premiums. Special editions, including personalized covers, corporate imprints, and excerpts, can be created in large quantities for special needs. For more information, contact the publisher.

We are always looking for people to write books on new and related subjects. If you have an idea for a book, please contact us at proposals@schifferbooks.com.

Contents

Foreword

The idea of writing a book on the MiG-29 came from my former Luftwaffe comrade Stefan. After our first visit to the Russian MAKS international aviation salon in Moscow in 1999, Stefan came up with the idea of upgrading his photo album, adding text about various types to some pages. Eventually, the idea developed that I should turn this into a book.

Until the appearance of this book there was no complete work about the MiG-29 in Germany, only some articles (though good) in magazines. And that is how this book came about. My time in the Bundeswehr gave me the opportunity to work on the unforgettable MiG-29 and gain insights that would have been difficult to come by outside the service. For me and many former comrades and civilians, it was a time that will always be fondly remembered.

The MiG-29 played an extremely important role for the Soviet Union, for this aircraft (and its big sister the Su-27) achieved a degree of maneuverability that had previously never been achieved, paired with capable radar equipment and weaponry. Many air forces later came to realize this for themselves in joint exercises. The MiG-29 left more than scratches in the self-consciousness of opposing pilots. The influence of the MiG-29 was felt in the development of new combat aircraft in the west and today, after thirty-eight years, it is still in service with various air forces, and thanks to upgrade packages it is still able to keep pace with competing designs from the west.

Acknowledgments

Of course I would like to express my thanks to those who helped in the creation of this book. I received a great deal of support, especially when it came to photographs. The first person I would like to thank is Stefan Gawlista, who provided many photographs taken during everyday operations by *JG 73*. My thanks to Peter Steiniger and Dr. Stefan Petersen as well, who generously provided photos and encouraged me to continue my search for illustrations. I even obtained photographic material from the manufacturers RAC MiG and UAC, and I am especially grateful to Mikhail Gorochov, who patiently answered my requests for photographs. And then there is Stefan Tonk, one of the engine technicians who was there for almost the MiG-29's entire career with the Bundeswehr. He wrote a chronicle containing many anecdotes and extraordinary events concerning the MiG-29's service with the Bundeswehr, some of which found a place in this book. Mariusz Wojciechowski provided invaluable assistance with his outstanding drawings, which enrich the book greatly. And of course there are those others who provided photos that helped round out this book. For these I would like to thank Chris Lofting, Vladislav Perminov, Weimeng, Markus Schrader, Adam Swechovski, Alexey Mityayev, Alexey Micheyev, Duro, Faisal Akram Ether, Babak Taghvaee, Petr Pirony, Theo van Vliet, Sergey Chaikovsky, Sina Atefi Pour, Bernie Condon, Dr. Frikkie Bekker, Matthias Gründer, Rob Schleiffert, Trevor Hall, Hugo Mambour, Eric Bannwarth, Frank Dombrink, Steve Brimley, and Patrick Bigel.

Andy Gröning
Potsdam, Germany
Autumn 2015

Early conventional design. *RAC MiG*

Chapter 1
Development History

The MiG-29's birth goes back to the late 1960s, when the Soviets evaluated combat experience from the Vietnam War. This revealed that at medium and long ranges, the F-4 Phantom was superior thanks to its radar and air-to-air missiles. In close-in combat, however, the smaller and more maneuverable MiG-21 was superior. The task at hand was to create a fighter combining the best features of both fighters. The key to this was extraordinary maneuverability, a high thrust-to-weight ratio and an advanced weapons system. It was decided to design a light (PLMI) and a heavy (PFI) fighter, as a long-range fighter was also needed. The PLMI was to achieve and maintain air superiority over friendly troops and the immediate battlefield area, whereas the PFI was designed to operate up to 180 miles deep into enemy territory. In addition to ground control, the new aircraft were also to possess a highly developed weapons system so as to be able to operate autonomously. And thus was created the MiG-29 and the Su-27. The MiG OKB (OKB is a Russian abbreviation for development office, MiG is derived from Mikoyan and Gurevich, founders of the MiG OKB) began work on the MiG-29 in 1970. Both the TsAGI (Central AeroHydrodynamic Institute) and the GosNIIAS (State Research Institute for Aircraft Systems) were both involved in the design from the beginning. While TsAGI was responsible for aerodynamic research, GosNIIAS worked on the aircraft's avionics. Both institutes were located in Zhukovsky near Moscow. Artem Mikoyan, founder of the MiG OKB, died on December 9, 1970, and Rostislav Belyakov took his place.

In 1972, the air forces issued a requirements catalogue for a fighter of the so-called fourth generation. The MiG OKB proposed two versions (an integral concept with a lift-producing fuselage and a rather conventional design), while the Sukhoi OKB also entered the race with two submissions, one an integral design and the other more conventional. The Yakovlev OKB also entered the competition

Rostislav Apollosovich Belyakov (1919–2014) chief designer of the MiG OKB from 1971 to 1997. *RAC MiG*

Alexander Andreyevich Chumachenko (1913–1995), chief designer of the MiG-29 from 1972 to 1982. *RAC MiG*

with two designs, the Yak-45M (light fighter) and the Yak-47 (long-range fighter). The latter designs proceeded no further than the design stage, however. After a thorough evaluation of the designs, the MiG OKB was directed to construct the PLMI (MiG-29), while the Sukhoi OKB was ordered to go ahead with the PFI (Su-27). There was much opposition within the design bureau, and opponents of the integral concept spoke out against it vociferously. They favored a more conventional layout, one version of which looked like a MiG-25 with a single vertical tail and redesigned fuselage and wing. This faction also believed that the conventional solution would be simpler to design and cheaper to produce. It was also claimed that the integral concept would not have the structural strength required for fighter-versus-fighter combat. Even some leading figures in the TsAGI opposed the integral concept.

While Alexander Chumachenko, deputy general designer and the engineer responsible for the MiG-29, saw the integral concept as the future, he wanted to play it safe. He therefore decided that both the supporters of the conventional and integral layouts should carry out design work, and submit it to the TsAGI for further analysis. The "integralists" invested much time and effort in comparing both designs and came to the conclusion that their variant was the better. They sent their findings to the TsAGI, which after carrying out its own tests concluded that only the integral design could provide the maneuverability demanded by the air force. Specifically, these showed that the conventional design's maximum angle of attack was twenty degrees. Even in close turning engagements the performance of this design was below requirements, as the airflow delivered by the outside air intake could not supply the engine with sufficient air. The disagreements between the two factions were not resolved until 1973–74, which delayed the entire project. The integral concept looked like this: the fuselage and wing formed a single, merged lifting body. The engines were housed in separate gondolas on the underside of the fuselage. A twin-engine configuration was chosen to provide a higher level of survivability in wartime and in peacetime prevent the loss of the fighter if one of its two engines failed. The first wind tunnel test with a wooden model of the MiG-29 took place in the TsAGI in 1973. The integral concept finally having won, construction of prototypes began. In the USA the new F-14 had entered service in 1972, and the F-14 in 1974. That same year the F-16 made its first flight and the F/A-18 was on the verge of taking to the air. The Soviets were thus facing the most modern western designs. Faced with this, the Soviet leadership initiated two MiG-29 programs in parallel, as they apparently feared falling behind. They wanted to get the MiG-29 to the units as

Various conventional
and integral designs.
Alexei Micheyev

quickly as possible, and as development of the new radar was lagging behind, they wanted an interim solution. The MiG-29A would therefore be fitted with an improved radar from the MiG-23ML or M, which was designated JANTAR. The MiG-29A would therefore have been a less effective version, for the new radar specially designed for the aircraft would be installed in the MiG-29 airframe at a later date (which in fact happened). In 1976, it was decided to abandon the MiG-29A program. The reason was simple: the JANTAR radar with all its components was too large for the airframe. Consideration was given to installing some avionics in a horseshoe-shaped fairing beneath the cockpit. This would have required a thickening of the leading edge root extension (LERX), which would have negatively affected the aerodynamics. The first four prototypes were built by the MiG OKB, which had its own factory (MMZ No. 155). The design bureau was assisted in building the prototypes by MMZ No. 30 (Znamya Truda), which later built the production aircraft. The first prototype left the factory in 1977 and ground testing began. The MiG-29 made its first flight on October 6, 1977. Aircraft 901 was flown by the OKB chief test pilot Alexander Fedotov. A total of fourteen prototypes were completed. The aircraft were numbered from 901 (the first prototype) to 925. As the MiG-29A was not built, the numbers 905–907 and 909–916 were not used in numbering the real MiG-29s. The only exception was No. 908. When the third prototype (903) was lost in a crash, the resulting gap had to be filled so as not to delay the test program. Therefore another prototype was built and given the number 908. Two aircraft were lost during flight testing as a result of engine failure. The two aircraft were 903 and 908, which were used for engine trials. 903 developed compressor trouble and Valeri Menitzki had to eject. One of 908's combustion chambers burned through and Alexander Fedotov was also forced to eject. Fedotov injured his back while ejecting and spent several months in the hospital as a result. In both cases flight control systems were damaged, rendering the aircraft uncontrollable. As testing progressed, cases of compressor damage became more frequent and it was discovered that the undercarriage threw up dirt that was sucked into the intakes. The intakes had shutters but failed to address the problem. For this reason the nosewheel leg was moved aft by approximately 4.5 feet and was also shortened. The new arrangement first appeared on the second prototype (No. 902) and has been a feature of all MiG-29s since then. In 1978, Fedotov began testing the aircraft's low-speed handling characteristics, flight behavior near the stall and recovery from a spin, and the TsAGI found

that ventral fins beneath the vertical tail surfaces were necessary to improve directional stability. These fins were present on all of the prototypes and the following seventy aircraft (pre-production and early production machines). They later disappeared and the vertical fin area was increased by the chord. An evaluation of the combat performances of other types in Afghanistan revealed that countermeasures were required against shoulder-fired SAMs (Stinger or Redeye). Chaff and flare dispensers were added as extensions of the tail fins. Each was able to hold thirty chaff or flare cartridges and also served as a boundary layer fence and combined with the larger tail fins improved directional stability. This configuration was tested on the sixth prototype (No. 917) and was not immediately used by the first production aircraft.

With the MiG-29 (plus the Su-27 and MiG-31) the Soviet Union had a weapons system that could compete against the latest western (primarily American) combat aircraft technology (the B-1, the F-14, the F-15, etc.).

After the Second World War and the beginning of the Cold War, the USSR was forced to shift the focus of its weapons research and industry, in part at the cost of fighter aircraft development. Given the touchy world political situation and the ongoing tensions between east and west, the development of atomic and rocket technology had top priority. The aircraft industry suffered as a result and in some areas the Soviets fell behind the west. The MiG-29 (and the Su-27/MiG-31) altered this drastically, for the three weapons systems subsequently demonstrated their enormous potential.

The MiG-29 officially entered service with the Soviet air forces in 1984. American spy satellites gave the west its first photos of the new type in 1979. Initially designated RAM-L, the aircraft was photographed at the Zhukovsky testing grounds. The USA thought that it was the town of Ramenskoye, which was close to Zhukovsky, hence the designation RAM-, which was also used for other types photographed there, as no other designations for the prototypes were known. The MiG-29 later received the NATO codename FULCRUM.

Early integral layout.

First prototype of the MiG-29 in 1977. *RAC MiG*

Summary of Prototypes

901 – Airframe load tests, performance and handling verification, dummy cannon, aerodynamic flight tests.

902 – Nosewheel leg moves aft 4.5 feet, IRST tests, first MiG-29 with integral wing tanks, testing of fire extinguishing system, tests of self-sealing fuel tanks, installation of GSh-301 cannon.

903 – Engine trials (crashed after compressor damage), rearrangement of the fuel system.

904 – Dynamic load tests.

908 – Engine trials (crashed after combustion chamber damage), modifications to the cannon armament.

917 – Larger vertical tail surfaces, verification of flight characteristics.

918 – Avionics and weapons systems tests, first MiG-29 with N-019 radar (without IRST however), first firing of the R-27R by the MiG-29, later used in trials for the MiG-29K program, unofficial designation MiG-29KVP.

919 – Radar tests, replacement of the analogue computer system with a digital one, first firing of the R-73 by the MiG-29, effects of vibration and high temperature on internal systems, measurement of loads associated with the use of cannon and missiles.

920 – Complete avionics suite fitted, tests at the Novaya Zemlya nuclear test site (tactical atomic weapons?).

921 – Completion of engine trials, including effects of cannon and missile use, testbed for RD-33K engine for the MiG-29M and K.

922 – Wind tunnel tests, weapons system tests.

923 – Tests with the IRST and navigation system, cannon tests, fire tests.

924 – Load tests, modification of engine nozzles and air intakes.

925 – Incorporation of all changes from the entire prototype test program.

The flight line at Lipetsk. *Theo van Vliet*

Chapter 2
In Service

On Home Soil

Series production of the MiG-29 began in 1982, even before the conclusion of official state acceptance trials! The first aircraft still had the ventral fins recommended by the TsAGI, as the institute believed that these improved a pilot's chances of successfully recovering from a spin. MiG itself also conducted tests and determined that these ventral fins were not necessary. This reduced weight and simplified installation and removal of the engine access panels. The first aircraft were officially handed over to the air force in 1983, the first unit to receive the new fighter being the 234th Guards Fighter Regiment in Kubinka. At that time there was no training version (UB) of the MiG-29, as the air force command and the manufacturer could not decide if this version was absolutely needed or not. Air Force Marshall Kutakov assigned his deputies to monitor conversion training of pilots onto the MiG-29. The MiG OKB also sent representatives to Kubinka, including chief designer Waldenberg and chief test pilot Fedotov. In the opinion of the MiG OKB, the training aircraft were not vitally needed for pilots with experience on other types. Two years earlier the MiG-29 had been demonstrated to then Defense Minister Ustinov at Kubinka. The MiG created an outstanding impression, something that could not be said of the Su-27, which was also demonstrated (this was the original T-10 variant, however, and not the T-10S known today). The 4th Combat and Training Center at Lipetsk was another of the first units to be equipped with the new MiG. This unit developed new tactics and maneuvers for the aircraft. There were even mock combats between the MiG-29 and the Su-27 (T-10S) and the test pilots found that the pilot's workload in aerial combat was somewhat less in the MiG-29 than the Su-27. The selected camouflage scheme consisted of two shades of grey on the upper surfaces and a single color on

Mikhail Romanovich Waldenberg (?? – 1998), chief designer of the MiG-29 from 1982–93. *RAC MiG*

the undersurfaces. Early production aircraft had a high percentage of components made of composite materials, including the engine air intakes and fairings, leading edges, tail fins, fuselage spine fairing, and wing tips (and obviously all panels over radio equipment). These composite components were responsible for two crashes in 1984, however. The cause was found to be hairline cracks in the panels caused by riveting during assembly. These cracks grew as the aircraft accumulated flying hours and components ultimately failed. The riveting procedure was changed and the rivet holes were now bored several processes earlier. These measures were supposed to prevent cracks from forming during riveting, however the problem did not go away, the riveting process still created problems. In one case one half of an air intake fairing separated during flight. At this point Pyotr Dementyev, the Minister of the Aviation Industry, intervened. He demanded that composite materials should no longer be used in critical flight components, and so the builder reverted to aluminum alloys. Mikoyan initially remained an advocate of composite materials, for if damage was found they were replaced with new parts until the next overhaul. These composite parts had originally been projected as long-life components and not ones that needed regular

replacement, and the aviation industry constantly had to deliver these still very expensive and technically challenging parts. They were incapable of delivering the required quantities to Mikoyan and turned to the aviation ministry for help. Dementyev again put his foot down and instructed Mikoyan to initially stop using the composite parts and instead produce them from aluminum. Only the radome, dielectric panels, some access panels, and the vertical fin skinning remained of composite materials, which were considered strong enough for these purposes.

The new fighter was not just assigned to units within the Soviet Union, however. In 1986, the MiG-29 entered service with the western group of Soviet forces in Germany but did not immediately replace the MiG-23 in all the wings stationed there. The mid-1980s saw a hardening of the relationship between the USSR and the USA and the period was characterized by armaments races. The Soviet Air Force therefore had to base its new fighters at well-considered locations. A blanket replacement of older types, such as the MiG-23, was not possible, as the new type had just entered production and was not available in sufficient numbers. The Soviets had to assume that the latest American combat aircraft like the F-15 and F-16 were already present in the NATO arsenal in much larger numbers. To the Soviet military leadership, this meant that a modernization of its combat aircraft and radar systems was urgently required. And then there was the war in Afghanistan—it was costing the USSR vast sums of money and materials and its effects were being felt all over the country. The catastrophic economic consequences of the war ultimately initiated the end of the USSR. Another aspect that is often overlooked is the Soviet Buran space shuttle program and its booster rockets. Both were outstanding products of the Soviet space industry that consumed vast sums of money, for a project that the Soviets did not need for their space program at that time.

For all of these reasons, economically it was simply impossible to produce sufficient MiG-29s to equip as many frontline units as possible with it in a short time. Consequently it was mainly delivered to strategically important units where hostilities were seen as a possibility. Such "main lines of resistance" ran along the western border of the Warsaw Pact, the southern and eastern flanks of the Soviet Union (particularly in the Ukrainian and White Russian Republics), the area surrounding the capital and important industrial areas.

The west received its first revealing photos and reports about the new Soviet Falcon in 1986, when six aircraft visited a Finnish unit at Rissala, Finland. The USSR had had close relations with that country for a long time, resulting

One of the first production aircraft, seen here still with ventral fins.

A MiG-29S at the testing center at Lipetsk. The purpose of the white stripes is to improve visibility during practice combat; the black anti-glare panel in front of the windscreen is already badly worn. *Theo van Vliet*

The raised periscope for the flight instructor in the rear cockpit is clearly visible in this photo of a MiG-29UB. Note the back anti-glare panel forward of the windscreen. *Theo van Vliet*

A pair of MiG-29 9.12s, each with a 400-gallon external fuel tank beneath the fuselage. *Vladislav Perminov*

in the export of defense technology (tanks, APCs, MiG-21s, etc.). The Soviets naturally hoped that they could also sell the MiG-29 to the Finns, to gain foreign exchange and tie Finland to the USSR politically to a certain degree. The MiG-29 was never exported to Finland, however, and the country later procured the American F/A-18.

In 1988, several MiG-29s were sent to Afghanistan to test the aircraft under operational conditions. There they were used both in the fighter role to protect the airspace and the fighter-bomber role against ground targets. These aircraft flew from bases close to Afghanistan in Central Asiatic Soviet republics. The fighters were painted in a modified camouflage scheme consisting of pale grey and green or various shades of brown. The pilots were briefed on the latest operational situation in Afghanistan before being sent there. This was carried out primarily at the

Special Center for Pilot Training in Mari (then the Turkmen Soviet Republic). The unit was established in 1970, during analysis of aerial combat in the Vietnam and Middle East wars. Analysts in the USSR came to realize that current practices and attitudes had become outdated and that they urgently needed to train their pilots. This base was selected because it enjoyed climatic conditions that permitted flying the whole year round (like Nellis AFB in Nevada). Among the pilots trained there were those who subsequently flew on the Egyptian side against the Israelis in MiG-21s and MiG-25s. Then in 1987, the unit received MiG-29s. Not every pilot in the Soviet Air Force was sent to Mari, only those whose piloting skills had stood out while serving in their units. When they returned they were supposed to pass on their new skills and knowledge to the other pilots of their units.

May 20, 1989, was a black day for the Soviet Air Force. That day pilot Alexander Zuyev defected to Turkey (Trabzon airfield) with his MiG-29. His actions were like something from a movie: he anesthetized the quick reaction pilots and technicians with sleeping pills, which he mixed into a cake, cut telephone lines and shot a sentry. Then he climbed into one of the MiG-29s assigned to the quick reaction flight and flew at an extreme low level to Turkey. Another quick reaction flight MiG-29 from his unit (one of the pilots had not eaten any of the cake) took off seven minutes later, followed a short time later by two interceptors from a neighboring unit. A surface-to-air missile unit was unable to track Zuyev because he was flying extremely low, precisely to avoid being located by radar. As Trabzon was less than ten minutes flying time from Zuyev's base, the first aircraft was unable to shoot him down while he was still in Soviet airspace. While the MiG-29 was returned the next day in keeping with an agreement between the two states, Turkey did not hand Zuyev over to the Soviet Union and he was later given asylum in the USA. During the Gulf War against Iraq, Zuyev advised the USA in matters concerning the MiG-29. A subsequent evaluation of the flight recorder by Soviet personnel revealed that Zuyev had twice attempted to fire his cannon at his own airfield. In his haste, however, he forgot to release the cannon safety.

By 2013, a total of approximately 1,400 single-seat (primarily the 9.13 version) and 200 two-seat MiG-29s were delivered. About 800 of these MiG-29s went to the Soviet Air Force. 500 of these were distributed in the interior of the country, 350 of them in the European part of the Soviet Union. Of these 350, about 230 aircraft were deployed in the Ukraine and White Russia. About 300 of the 800 were based in East Germany (about 250) and Czechoslovakia and Hungary. The number of MiGs held by the units varied considerably. On average each wing had about thirty MiGs, though in some cases the number was forty or even higher. The period from the early 1990s until the beginning of the twenty-first century were difficult days for all of Russia and its successor states. Of course the military and the air force were also affected, especially by a shortage of fuel, which the military now had to purchase at high prices, and the number of hours the pilots flew in their machines dropped to a low point. In the mid-1990s, fighter pilots on average logged a maximum of twenty flying hours per year, while western pilots as a rule flew six or seven times as many hours per year. While this may have been enough for experienced pilots to master their aircraft, this inadequate experience often ended in death, or at least a crash. As a result the air force's operational readiness sank to a point where the question arose as to whether it could defend the

The covers have been removed from the chaff-flare dispensers. This was only done on the ground when their use was expected. *Vladislav Perminov*

The special finish worn by aircraft of the Falcon display team based at Lipetsk. *Chris Lofting*

MiG-29UB of the test center at Domna, near the Mongolian-Chinese border. *Eric Bannwarth*

country in the event of war. 1993 was the year with the most crashes, and of thirty-three Russian Air Force aircraft that went down, twenty-two were MiG-29s! Six of these crashes were attributed to technical failures. Meanwhile the situation improved thanks to restructuring, reforms, and in particular the strengthening Russian economy.

In 2008, there were two crashes in rapid succession in a Siberian unit, and once again technical shortcomings were to blame. All 291 Russian Air Force MiG-29s were subsequently grounded. An investigation revealed that cracks in the area between the base of the tail fins and the airframe had again developed. Possible causes were the simplified and in part poor maintenance in the period after the USSR. Aircraft were also stored outside for long periods with minimal protection against the harsh Russian climate, which opened the door to corrosion. At least as bad was the fact that the Russian Air Force used large quantities of aggressive deicing fluids. These were necessary to deal with the severe Russian winters, but why materials were not used which did not attack the airframe could only be justified by cost—less aggressive deicing materials were available in commercial aviation for example. As many as 200 machines were affected by the problem to varying degrees. The MiG-29 is operated by five fighter regiments,

in Domna (near Mongolia), Sernograd and Millerovo (area around Rostov on Don, Black Sea), and in Kursk and Kubinka (Moscow area). It is also operated by fighter training regiments in Kuchevskaya, Armavi (both in the Rostov on Don area), and Borisoglebsk and Michurinsk (both in the Kursk area). Finally there is also the Training/Test Flying Regiment in Pipetsk (Kursk area), and the Central Combat Training Regiment in Astrakhan (near the Caspian Sea).

As described at length in the chapters on modernized MiG-29 versions, many technical advances have been used to update the original model. Because of the economic situation in the Russian Air Force these did not take place until 2008. The acquisition of modern variants was in fact not of the air force's choosing, but resulted from the cancellation of a contract for the delivery of MiG-29 SMT 9.19 fighters to Algeria in 2006. The apparent reason was technical shortcomings with the aircraft that had been

SMY 9.19 wearing the Russian Air Force's new camouflage scheme. Russian aircraft are now again wearing the Red Star as a nationality symbol, although now with a white-blue border. Also new are the light strips (vertical tail and fuselage nose), which are helpful during formation flight in darkness. *Chris Lofting*

Joint exercise involving Russian Air Force SMT 9.19, and French Mirage F1CR fighters at Tver, Nizhni Novgorod in 2013. *Patrick Bigel*

delivered, in which secondhand parts had allegedly been used. This seemed rather unbelievable, as Algerian experts had already accepted fifteen aircraft and had made no complaints. It was suspected that rivalries in the Algerian army command were responsible for the retraction of the agreement. Ultimately, the fifteen MiG-29 SMTs that had been delivered were returned to Russia on the condition that other defense contracts would be negotiated. The aircraft were given to the Russian Air Force, making them the first modernized MiG-29s for Russia since the collapse of the USSR. Meanwhile further MiG-29 SMTs were acquired for the air force and there are now forty-four aircraft of this type in service. Incidentally the UBTs in service with the Russian Air Force have refueling probes, but they are not connected to the fuel system. The probes are used only for pilot training. One also finds no photos of "true" UBTs with the typical enlarged spinal bulge. In 2012, a court in Moscow convicted several heads of companies accused of delivering used or substandard parts. Previously, in 2007, prison sentences had been handed down for delivering substandard parts to Poland. To what degree MiG was responsible for failing to recognize that subcontractors were delivering substandard parts remains an open question.

It was frequently heard from government circles that the MiG-35 should be purchased for the Russian military. This was put off several times. The reason may again have been lack of funds, however the MiG-35 is the technological end product of the MiG-29 family, including the SMT. Official bodies also do not believe the armaments industry is in a position to begin producing the aircraft in sufficient numbers. Ultimately, existing MiG-29s can be modified to SMT standard, but not to MiG-35 standard. The SMT shares certain features with the MiG-35 and is by no means a stopgap. It must be remembered, however, that the MiG-29s already in service have high airframe times, even if this can be extended by structural modifications.

In 2012, the Russian Defense ministry decided to procure the latest MiG-29 K/KUB for its aircraft carrier *Admiral Kuznetsov* and replace the obsolescent Su-33. The contract covered twenty MiG-29 Ks and four MiG-29 KUB. In 2014, a decision was also made to procure sixteen SMTs for the home air force, to be delivered by 2016. In 2015, there were close to 190 MiG-29s in service, from the 9.12 to the 9.19.

At MiG consideration has been given to how to employ combat aircraft if their runways are damaged by enemy air attack. An assessment was made of the Allied air attacks in the first Gulf War. The runways that had been bombed had craters that were 980 feet apart. A solution therefore had to be found how to use these sections of undamaged runway. This was made possible by a sort of ski jump, similar to the launch deck of the *Admiral Kuznetsov* and the British *Invincible* Class carriers. The structure consists of several parts and weighs just over twenty-two tons. When assembled, the ramp is 46 feet long and 30 inches high. It is loaded onto trucks and can be assembled by three technicians in about forty-five minutes. In 1997, a MiG-29 took off from such a mobile ski jump after a roll of just 650 feet.

A MiG-29 with internal fuel and four air-to-air missiles (2 x R-27, 2 x R-73) can safely get airborne after a takeoff run of about 820 feet. The ramp is suitable for aircraft with gross weights up to 35,275 pounds. This design enables takeoff roll to be reduced by a factor of 2.5. The problem of landing has not yet been solved, however, for a shortened landing roll is not possible. But in this way aircraft are not tied to the ground and can at least be safely flown away or be sent on combat sorties.

Of note are two records which show once again the performance potential of the MiG-29 design: on April 26, 1995, test pilot Roman Taskayev climbed to 90,091 in a standard MiG-29 (12–16 ton class). And in May 1995, another MiG-29 climbed to more than 82,020 feet with a 1.10-ton payload.

SMT 9.19 with
550-pound
practice bomb
in the
foreground.
*Sergey
Chaikovsky*

SMY 9.19 with
operational
R-27 and R-73
air-to-air
missiles.
*Sergey
Chaikovsky*

9.13 with R-27 and R-73 missile simulators. *Sergey Chaikovsky*

MiG-29UB with refueling probe. In addition to the Red Star, the legend VVS Rossiya (Russian Air Force) appears on the vertical tail. *Sergey Chaikovsky*

SMT 9.19 with B-8 rocket pods, each containing twenty 3.5-inch rockets. A country identification code appears beneath the Red Star on the vertical tail. *Patrick Bigel*

SMT 9.19 with practice bombs under the wings. *Sergey Chaikovsky*

The engine air intakes are straight designs, consequently the compressor blades make an excellent reflector for enemy radars. *Sergey Chaikovsky*

The wheel hubs are typically green on Russian fighter aircraft. The nosewheel stone guard is clearly visible. *Sergey Chaikovsky*

SMT 9.19 during takeoff. The "hunchback" spine of the 9.19 is clearly visible. *Sergey Chaikovsky*

SMT 9.19 with the marking VVS Rossia (Russian Air Force) but with no nationality code, probably applied for domestic air displays such as the traditional victory parade over Red Square on May 9. *Sergey Chaikovsky*

Flight line with thrust deflectors behind the MiG-29s. *Sergey Chaikovsky*

The 16th Air Army in East Germany

The 16th Air Army was formed during the Battle of Stalingrad in 1942. It took part in many combat actions and probably became the largest tactical air unit in the former Soviet Union. After 1945, as the Cold War grew in intensity, it was stationed on the soil of what became the German Democratic Republic (GDR: East Germany). The first MiG-29s were sent to the 16th Air Army in 1986. In 1994, a MiG-29 became the last Russian warplane to leave German soil.

A number of first series aircraft with ventral fins served with the 16th Air Army, but also 9.13 series aircraft. In case of a confrontation with NATO, the type was capable of delivering nuclear weapons, specifically the RN-40 and RN-42 tactical nuclear bombs, each with an explosive force of 30 kilotons. These bombs are known to have been permanently available to the wing in Altenburg, and all other units with the exception of the unit at Eberswalde–Finow at times had a nuclear weapons dump.

Conversion from the MiG-23 to the MiG-29 did not take place in all units simultaneously. Deliveries of the MiG-29UB trainer failed to keep pace with requirements, and as a result some units of the 16th Air Army in East Germany used the MiG-23UB to convert to the MiG-29.

With the exception of the one at Eberswalde–Finow, the MiG-29 units were stationed in the northern part of the GDR (north–south axis). All of the fighter and fighter-bomber wings of the East German Nationale Volksarmee (NVA) were based in the eastern part of the country, and also distributed north to south. Whether the Soviet high command did not trust the NVA to successfully defend against NATO units coming from West Germany in the event of war is hypothetical. The MiG-29 units of the 16th Air Army in East Germany formed the first defensive-offensive ring, assuming that the former East and West Germany had become a battlefield between the two superpowers, the USSR and the USA.

MiG-29 9.13 fighters on the flight line at Eberswalde–Finow in 1993. One power box supplies two parking spaces with power; no other ground equipment or starter trucks are needed to power the aircraft. *Hugo Mambour*

IN SERVICE

6th Fighter Division

31st Regiment Falkenberg 1989–93; 32 aircraft,
(Sernograd, Russia)
85th Regiment Merseburg 1986–91; 30 aircraft,
(Starokonstantinov, Ukraine)
968th Fighter Regiment Altenburg 1989–92; 30 aircraft,
(Lipetsk, Russia)

16th Fighter Division

33rd Regiment Wittstock 1985–94; 39 aircraft,
(Andreapol, Russia)
773rd Fighter Regiment Riebnitz–Damgarten 1989–94,
25 aircraft,
(Andreapol, Russia)
787th Regiment Finow 1989–93; 30 aircraft,
(Ros, White Russia)

126th Fighter Division

35th Regiment Zerbst 1988–92; 28 aircraft,
(Zerdevka, Russia)
73rd Regiment Köthen 1988–91; 36 aircraft,
(Chaykovka, Russia)

In fact the MiG-29, the Soviets' latest and most modern frontline fighter, entered service there, while the Su-27, with its great range, was stationed on Polish soil. The Soviet air force also posted other MiG-29 units in Hungary (about 100 aircraft of the 36th Air Army) and Czechoslovakia (twelve MiGs of the 131st Mixed Aviation Division in Milovice), though in smaller numbers than in East Germany. The types were usually flown three times per week, and the airfield radars had an extremely negative effect on television reception in the area. Overland supersonic flights were also a normal part of flying operations.

On September 14–15, 1993, two aircraft from the wing at Wittstock were involved in an accident. The two MiG-29s were assigned to an air-to-air cannon firing exercise. Just before takeoff one of the MiG-29s was declared unserviceable and the pilot climbed into another aircraft, however he failed to notice that this aircraft's cannon system was set to live-fire mode. During the mock combat the aircraft's pilot fired on the other MiG-29 with live ammunition, inflicting serious damage. The stricken MiG crashed. Wreckage from the first aircraft struck the second MiG-29 and it also went down. Both pilots ejected and survived.

After the Soviet withdrawal from East Germany from 1991 to 1994, most of the aircraft were assigned to Russian bases, while those at Merseburg went back to the Ukraine

The symbol on the fuselage nose is a decoration for the ground personnel, as the aircraft has achieved a high standard of maintenance. This is a 9.13 with standard 300-gallon underwing fuel tanks. *Hugo Mambour*

Final checks just prior to takeoff, Falkenberg 1993. *Eric Bannwarth*

9.12 of the unit from Wittstock. *Frank Dombrink*

The flight line at Falkenberg in 1993, here with Ural starter truck. *Eric Bannwarth*

and those from Eberswalde-Finow went to White Russia. A total of 250 aircraft were in service with eight regiments. The locations in bracket indicates the bases to which the aircraft were flown after leaving Germany.

For the soldiers and civilians of the 16th Air Army (indeed for all members of the GSSD, or Group of Soviet Forces in Germany), the future in their homeland was uncertain. The USSR no longer existed, and Russia, whose economy was in crisis, had other worries than operating its armed forces on the same scale as the former Soviet Union. Returning units operating older types were disbanded or sent to other home bases. Personnel strengths were cut drastically and soon after returning home many units found themselves with nothing to do. A much more serious problem was providing living space for the 560,000 personnel who

had come home. In more than a few cases pilots slept in the helicopters they had flown home, because there were no quarters for them or because there was no one willing to assume responsibility for finding them. Others had to sleep in tents and began growing their own food.

Happily, this is now part of the past and once again conditions in the air force have returned to near normal, even though the modernization and pay in the Russian armed forces are generally lagging behind what has been promised by the politicians.

Strizhi Air Display Squadron

This squadron was officially formed in 1991, and was created from the 2nd Squadron of the 234th Guards Aviation Regiment in Kubinka, which was established in 1952, and given the name Strizhi (Swift). During the Great Patriotic War Kubinka was a base from which units took part in the air battles over Moscow. Units from Kubinka also took part in the Korean War.

The formation of a group for the use and development of advanced aerobatics began in the mid-1980s, shortly after the MiG-29 entered service. The Swifts made their air show debut in France in 1992, on the fiftieth anniversary of the French Normandie-Nieman Squadron. Since then the squadron has given countless displays at air shows in Russia and abroad. The color scheme worn by the unit's aircraft has evolved from the original white and blue to a white, blue, and red scheme. As previously mentioned, the squadron's home base is Kubinka, near Moscow. Kubinka is home to the testing and air display center and a fighter wing. In addition to the Swifts, the Russkiye Vityasi (Russian Knights) unit and its Su-27s are also stationed there.

Before their arrival in France, the Swifts first appeared outside Russia during a friendship visit to Uppsala in Sweden. Foreign and no less famous visitors have also appeared at Kubinka, including the Americans and their US Navy display team the Blue Angels flying F/A-18s. In addition to the obligatory appearances at the MAK air shows at Zhukovsky, the Swifts have travelled to every part of the world except Australia. In 2000, the unit was transferred to Andreapol. Both pilots and ground personnel are members of the demonstration and testing center and are not attached to any permanent unit. In addition to aerobatics, the pilots also undergo combat training.

MiG-29UB in original finish at Sperenberg during the 16th Air Army's departure from East Germany in 1994. *Hugo Mambour*

One of the Swifts' UBs in the special finish worn
by the aircraft since 2006. *RAC MiG*

A Polish MiG on jacks in the maintenance hangar at Malbork.
RAC MiG

Chapter 3
Abroad

By the mid-1990s, about 500 MiG-29s were exported to foreign air forces or transferred to states that succeeded the Soviet Union. It was the policy of the Soviet Union (not only where the MiG-29 was involved) to export less technologically advanced versions of weapons systems. The level of sophistication differed depending on the nation involved. Libya, for example, operated a much less advanced version of the MiG-23 than did East Germany (which received the MiG-23ML). The effectiveness of the aircraft's radar, in particular, was downgraded, resulting in less effective weapons systems. This was done to prevent the western powers from gaining access to the latest Soviet defense technology. The USSR's trust in some of its Warsaw Pact defense partners was also less marked than in others, which was reflected in the MiG-29s exported to those nations. After the collapse of the Soviet Union this changed fundamentally and it is not the latest versions of the MiG-29 that are offered for sale abroad. The reason is clear: especially in its first decade, Russia was in no position to purchase new military equipment for its armed forces or carry out modernization programs. The MiG OKB and the factory that built the aircraft were thus forced to look for customers outside Russia. Export was the order of the day if the MiG OKB was to survive. Meanwhile the complex broke up into individual concerns, the MiG OKB as a development and design bureau, MAPO as the actual manufacturing company, and VPK MAPO as MAPO's organizational unit. Later, under the leadership of Nikolai Nikitin, the three independent companies were brought back together under the title RSK MiG. Since 2006, almost all of the former OKBs of the Soviet Union have been combined into a single entity (UAC). MiG, as part of UAC, is now called Russian Aircraft Corporation RAC MiG.

Algeria

From 2000 to 2001, Algeria received MiG-29s from White Russia and the Ukraine. After several years in service, it became apparent that without the Russian manufacturer, technical support and the provision of spares were impossible. The country turned to Russia, which offered to provide the SMT 9.19. The aircraft were delivered, however the contract was cancelled. In 2013, there were still about thirty aircraft in service with the Algerian air force.

Azerbaijan

In the period leading up to the breakup of the USSR, tactical combat and reconnaissance aircraft were based in the Republic of Azerbaijan, mainly Su-24s, Su-25s, and MiG-25s. Modern aircraft such as the MiG-29 and Su-27 were not in the inventory of Azerbaijani units at that time. The Ukraine was ready to sell the country MiG-29s,

but Azerbaijan did not want heavily used machines. It wanted aircraft that had been modernized to extend their operational life with the addition of modern systems. Ukrainian companies outfitted the MiGs with a satellite navigation system, the aircraft's radar was improved to extend its range, and the aircraft were modified to enable them to use the Kh-29 television-guided missile. A total of twelve single-seat fighters were modernized and two two-seaters were used for training. The aircraft were delivered between 2005 and 2007. An additional twenty-four MiG-29s were subsequently procured, primarily from the Ukraine.

Bangladesh

In 2000, the country received six single-seat and two two-seat versions of the MiG-29, the most modern fighters in the air force of Bangladesh. The first pilots for the MiG-29 were trained in Russia, later test pilots from RAC MiG assisted in training additional pilots in Bangladesh. Some pilots were also trained on simulators in Malaysia. Meanwhile a number of aircraft underwent basic overhaul

The MiG-29s of the Bangladesh Air Force wear a camouflage scheme which must probably be very effective over the sea. The aircraft seen here is carrying practice bombs under its wings. The unit of the Bangladesh Air Force is based at Hazrat Shahjalai International Airport in Dhaka. *Faisal Akram Ether*

in the Ukraine. Mikoyan made an offer to Malaysia to modernize its MiG-29s, probably on the basis of the SMT program, however no contract was signed. The pilots sang the aircraft's praises, as their MiG-29s represented a quantum leap over the A-5s and F-7s (Chinese copies of the MiG-19 and MiG-21) they had previously flown. The aircraft's handling, powerful engines, and radar, in particular, made a great impression.

Bulgaria

Bulgaria was the last eastern European nation to equip with the MiG-29, receiving a total of twenty-two aircraft in 1990. In the years that followed there were several negotiations with Russia and internal debates as to whether in the future the country would buy Russian or western military equipment. One side argued that purchasing Russian equipment would further increase dependence on that nation and make entry into NATO difficult or impossible. The other side argued that they could of course purchase used F-16s or F/A-18s, which would also not be cheap. This would require the replacement of the entire ground infrastructure, which would incur further costs. And of course they would then be dependent on the west.

Ultimately the collapsed Bulgarian economy meant that no new aircraft were purchased. Funds were so short that maintaining the aircraft became a problem and finally, by the late 1990s, spares were in such short supply that almost the entire MiG-29 fleet had to stay on the ground. Just six aircraft were fit to fly.

In 2006, a contract was signed with RAC MiG to make sixteen MiG-29s flyable and increase airframe life to 4,000 hours. The Bulgarian company TEREM carried out the necessary work on the airframes in cooperation with MiG, while work on engines and avionics was carried out in Russia.

In contrast to East Germany, the Bulgarians used a camouflage scheme made up of several shades of grey. *Chris Lofting*

CSSR, Czech Republic, and Slovakia

In 1989, the former CSSR received twenty MiG-29s. In 1992, the CSSR broke up, resulting in the Czech Republic and Slovakia. Each nation received ten MiG-29s. The Czechs decided to trade their aircraft for eleven Polish W-3 helicopters; however the Slovaks kept their MiG-29s and in 1994–95, acquired fourteen more aircraft from Russia. Like the German MiGs, the Slovakian MiG-29s were often used in comparative trials against NATO types. These did not assume the dimensions of the German Luftwaffe, but the pilots of the Slovakian MiG-29s also earned the respect of their opponents. As the MiG-29s were approaching the end of their service lives, the Slovakian air force and government decided to upgrade twelve aircraft with Russian support. The modernization deal was concluded with MiG in 2004 and was valued at about 70 million US dollars, of which about 50 million was settled from the Russian debt to Slovakia. As Slovakia was by then already a member of NATO, the upgrade focused on the installation of communications and navigation equipment. This was required to allow the Slovakian MiGs to operate with other NATO combat aircraft. A new IFF system by the British company BAE Systems (AN/APX 113 in the single-seat aircraft, AN/APX 117 in the two-seaters) was installed, as was a radio from Rockwell Collins (AN/ARC-210), a modern navigation/ILS system (AN/ARN-147 VOR/ILS) and a digital TACAN receiver. In the cockpit, the old monochrome display was replaced by a Russian liquid crystal display. This provides better indications from the radar and the optical sensors. A digital LCD control panel was fitted on the front side of the HUD, making for more comfortable operation and indication of some systems. Airframe life was extended to 4,000 flying hours. Pavel Vlasov, MiG's chief test pilot, made the first flight of a MiG-29AS in 2005. A total of ten single-seat and two two-seat MiG-29s were converted at the Slovak Air Force maintenance facility in Trencin and are expected to remain in service until 2015. All aircraft are based at Sliac.

A so-called digital camouflage scheme, similar to that worn on American service uniforms, was applied to two aircraft. The aircraft finished this way were used mainly for display purposes but were also used to evaluate the scheme's effectiveness. The scheme is very costly to apply, consequently not all aircraft are thus finished, the majority having conventional camouflage.

Slovakian MiG-29AS converted to NATO standard, recognizable by the blade antenna aft of the cockpit.
Duro

MiG-29UB of the Slovakian Air Force wearing a special finish on the occasion of a Tiger Meet. Beyond it are a single-seat MiG-29, L-39 Albatros, and British Hawks.

Aircraft of the unit from Sliac wearing the special
Tiger Meet paint scheme. Here the aircraft is
carrying the R-60 short-range AAM. *RAC MiG*

This MiG-29UB has been converted to NATO standard. All Slovakian MiG-29s are based at Sliac. *Duro*

This MiG-29 is pulling high g loads while releasing flares. *Adam Svechovski*

The fusion of the wings and fuselage—the so-called integral layout—is very obvious in this photo. *Markus Schrader*

The Slovaks were the first to use digital camouflage on aircraft. The original aircraft of the Czechoslovakian Air Force were camouflaged in shades of brown and green, similar to the scheme used by the East Germans. *Adam Svechovski*

Cuba

Cuba received twelve single-seat and two two-seat MiG-29s prior to the fall of the Soviet Union. The country actually planned to acquire significantly more aircraft (up to forty), but the financial situation curtailed further purchases. During Soviet times, Gorbachev also wanted to ease the political climate between his country and the USA and so there were no further deliveries. The Cuban aircraft were painted in different camouflage schemes. Some of the aircraft (especially the single-seaters) were finished in a scheme of browns and greens, while the two-seaters flew mainly in a scheme made up of shades of grey. After the collapse of the eastern block it became very difficult for the Cubans to maintain the standard they had achieved. Serviceability was reduced to a handful of MiGs, and without favorable offers from Russia the future of the MiG-29 in Cuba appears to be very bleak.

Eritrea

Between 1998 and 2001, Eritrea received eight MiG-29s, two of which were converted to SMT 9.18 standard. Ukrainian instructors were in the country to familiarize pilots with the MiG-29, which also leads to the conclusion that the aircraft had come from the Ukraine. The Eritrean MiG-29s saw combat at the end of the 1990s, including ground attacks against Ethiopian troops. The cause of the conflict was border disputes between the two neighboring countries. In 1999, there was an air engagement between Eritrean MiG-29s and Ethiopian Su-27s.

Four Eritrean MiG-29s flew an intercept mission along the border with Ethiopia. Their target was two Ethiopian Su-27s, which were suspected of being in Eritrean airspace. The Su-27s spotted the approaching MiGs and turned away. Suddenly, they detected approaching missiles. According to reports they were R-27 air-to-air missiles. None struck the Su-27s, however. The Su-27s accepted battle and fired missiles, again R-27s, at the MiGs. Again none of the missiles found their target. Finally, one of the MiG-29s was shot down by a Su-27, probably using an R-73. Just one day later there was another combat between an Eritrean MiG-29 and an Ethiopian Su-27. While escorting MiG-21s on a ground attack mission, the Su-27 spotted a lone aircraft. This turned out to be an unarmed MiG-29UB. The Su-27 signaled the pilot of the MiG, indicating that he should land at an Ethiopian airfield. When he refused to do so, the Su-27 fired two missiles. The MiG-29 was able to evade these but was shot down by cannon fire from the Su-27. It is interesting that the Su-27 was allegedly flown by a female pilot, Capt. Aster Tolossa. Because of the Ethiopian Air Force's air superiority there were no further engagements between its Su-27s and the Eritrean Air Force's MiGs.

Hungary

Hungary was the last European country to receive the MiG-29, obtaining twenty-two single-seat and six two-seat aircraft in 1995–96. The delivery cost was written off against Russia's foreign debt and had a value of approximately 800 million US dollars. After about a decade of service just twelve aircraft remained on active

service. Two MiGs were lost in crashes, the rest were placed in storage or served as sources of spare parts. In 2001, some aircraft were fitted with GPS equipment and NATO-capable IFF systems. The MiGs were based at Kecskemet. The last Hungarian MiG-29s were retired in 2010. The country has since leased Swedish JAS-39 Gripen aircraft and these will most likely remain in service for a long time.

India

India's air force became the first after that of the Soviet Union to operate the MiG-29 in 1986. The first inquiries about procurement were made in the early 1980s. The delivery of F-16s to the country's mortal enemy Pakistan may have hastened inquiries about the MiG-29. It was feared that the acquisition of modern fighters by Pakistan might place India at a disadvantage in the event of renewed hostilities. In 1984, an agreement was reached for the purchase of forty-four aircraft at a unit cost of 11 million US dollars. License production was discussed but never took place. A total of eighty aircraft was procured between 1986 and 1997 (seventy-two single-seat and eight two-seat

Prototype of the MiG-29UPG. The larger hunchback spine is clearly visible, while the horizontal pale stripes on the vertical stabilizer are reinforcements in response to the formation of cracks found earlier.
Weimeng

Production MiG-29UPG in service with the Indian Air Force, recognizable by the antennas of the Eloka systems on the wings and vertical tail surfaces. *Alexey Mityaev*

versions). Initially, the Indians were dissatisfied that they received the simplified 9.12B version. In 1996–97, several MiG-29s were modified to carry external fuel tanks beneath the wings, the range of weapons was expanded (improved versions of the R-27 AAM), the radar was now capable of engaging two targets simultaneously, and maximum airframe and engine life was extended.

The MiGs were assigned to three units, two in Poona and a third in Adampur. In 2008, a contract was signed between India and Russia for modernization of the Indian MiG-29 fleet. This contract envisaged conversion to MiG-29UPG standard of four single-seaters by MiG and two two-seaters by SOKOL. The remaining fifty-six aircraft would be converted by the Indian Air Force itself, using components and assemblies delivered by Russia. In 2010, the first of the modified aircraft made its maiden flight in the hands of test pilot Mikhail Belyayev. The centerpiece of the program was the modernization of the weapons system, layout of the cockpit, and the fuel system. An important aspect of the weapons system modernization was the new Zhuk M2E radar. While it was not a phased array radar like that of the MiG-35, it was capable of using the radar signature to determine if a target was a fighter,

a bomber, or a helicopter. Individual aircraft in a formation could be attacked if they were not closer than 100 feet in formation. An aircraft type could even be identified by a known radar signature. If it was the signature of a new type, it could be saved and later analyzed (a similar process had long been used to identify submarine types by their noise signature). In addition, the OELS targeting system was improved so that the IR sensor could locate aircraft flying in front up to twenty-eight miles away and aircraft on reciprocal course at up to 9.3 miles. Also new was a thermal image sensor. Retained were the laser range finder, which could now measure distances up to 9.3 miles, and the TV sensor. This optical targeting system is also installed in the MiG-35 and MiG-29K/KUB. The cockpit is now dominated by liquid crystal displays. The navigation system is in part based on satellite navigation—this and modern communications systems plus a helmet sight consisting of French, Indian, and Israeli components. Additional flare and chaff dispensers are fitted beneath the wings. A rearwards-facing antenna fairing, part of the electronic warfare (EW) system, is fitted in the root of the left tail fin. With respect to the fuel system, the same path was followed as the MiG-29SMT 9.19, which was originally developed

Indian Air Force MiG-29UPG
refueling from a Russian MiG-29K
9.41. *RAC MiG*

for Algeria and is now in use by the Russian Air Force. On this version the fuselage spine wads enlarged to accommodate a larger fuel tank. This is the same as that of the SMT 9.19 version and holds 251 gallons of fuel. On the left side of the fuselage beneath the cockpit is an external, extendable refueling probe. Range on internal fuel has been raised to 1,118 miles, while with three externals tanks it is 1,864 miles. According to MiG, use of the shorter dorsal tank compared to the 9.17 variants is intended to reduce the danger of an engine fire should pieces of wreckage penetrate the dorsal tank, in case of structural failure for example. Another reason for the shortened dorsal tank may be the associated ease of technical access to equipment drive units. Maximum airframe time was increased from 2,500 to 3,500 hours, which for the Indian Air Force is equivalent to forty years of operation. Weapons load is almost 9,920 pounds. The modernization is valued at about one million US dollars.

In 1999, there was an armed clash between India and Pakistan, after Pakistan occupied part of the Kashmir. India launched an offensive against the Pakistani forces, with MiG-29s providing top cover for ground forces and fighter-bombers. Armed with medium- and long-range AAMs, the MiG-29s kept the Pakistani F-16s at arm's length, as these had only short-range air-to-air missiles. The Pakistan Air Force's F-16s were thus unable to prevent the Indians from attacking their ground forces. In some cases, the MiG-29s locked onto the F-16s to demonstrate that they had them in their sights.

Iran

Iran acquired the MiG-29 from the Soviet Union prior to the ferrying of Iraqi MiG-29s to Iran, this taking place in 1990. The Iran–Iraq War had ended two years earlier. Iraq was already operating the type, and Iran did not want to lag behind. The bringing down of the American-supported regime by the revolution also put an end to the delivery of western technology, especially from the USA, from which Iran had purchased dozens of F-14As. Iran had to seek a new partner and this was found in the Soviet Union. Initial deliveries from the USSR consisted of twelve single-seaters and two two-seaters, and later deliveries increased this figure to about thirty aircraft. Moldavia also sought to sell its MiG-29s to Iran, but these aircraft were the nuclear-capable 9.13 version. International pressure stopped the sale from going through, and the USA bought the aircraft to keep them off the market. Iran had meanwhile modernized

some of its MiGs, adding refueling probes and updating elements of the radio equipment. This work was carried out by Iranian industry. Iran's MiG-29s are based at Tabriz.

Iraq

The first MiG-29s were exported to Iraq in 1987 and deliveries ultimately totaled between thirty and forty-one aircraft, including six two-seaters. The aircraft were stationed around the capital city of Bagdad. Following the Iraqi invasion of Kuwait in 1990, there was a buildup of American forces in Saudi Arabia. MiG-29s were subsequently transferred to the border there. When the Gulf War broke out in 1991, in the first days an Iraqi MiG-29 pilot succeeded in hitting an F-111 and a B-52 in the air. Another Iraqi MiG-29 pilot shot down a British Tornado GR.1. On the other hand up to eight MiG-29s were shot down by the Allies. These numbers—like all such war reports—must be evaluated with caution. When it became apparent that the Allied forces were far superior to the Iraqi Air Force, about 140 Iraqi combat aircraft, including about nine MiG-29s, were flown to Iran to prevent their destruction. The Iraqi pilots were interned in Iran and the aircraft (when possible) were delivered to the Iranian Air Force. This was a very noteworthy step by the Iranians, as the bitterly fought Iran–Iraq War had ended just three years earlier. The sanctions that followed the war made it impossible for Iraq to maintain the serviceability of the remaining fifteen aircraft. After the Second Gulf War in 2005, Iraq had no MiG-29s left on strength.

Israel

According to rumors, Israel acquired three MiG-29s in 1997. These may have come from the USA, which had previously purchased the Moldavian MiGs. As Syria, Iraq and Iran were then flying the type (Iran and Syria still are), for Israel it was a perfect opportunity to closely examine the MiG. The automatic landing system and automatic recovery from dangerous flight situations were seen as very helpful. Also praised were the aircraft's thrust-to-weight ratio, maneuverability in close combat and its helmet sight. The Israelis were also positively surprised by the aircraft's radar and infrared tracking system. Important components and systems of the MiG-29 were reliable but as simple as possible in design. Starting of the engines, for

Iranian Air Force MiG-29. The missing engine fairing panels suggest an engine test run. *Sina Atefi Pour*

Iranian components are recognizable behind the cockpit and beneath the fuselage nose. *Babak Taghvaee*

example, was found to be very uncomplicated. There were also few technical problems during testing. Fully exploiting the MiG's potential required a great deal of work in the cockpit, however, and some tactical information considered important by the Israelis was not displayed. All in all, when it came to performance in close-in combat, the Israeli Air Force put the MiG-29 on a par with the F-15 and F-16, and even found it superior in certain aspects.

Kazakhstan

No Soviet MiG-29s were based on the territory of the new state of Kazakhstan. Mainly based there were Tu-95 bombers carrying guided nuclear weapons. These nuclear bombers had no role either in the country's military doctrine or its budgetary planning. As a nuclear power, however, Russia was very interested in these aircraft, and the Russians proposed trading several dozen Su-27s and MiG-29s for the Tu-95s. And so in 1995, the first MiG-29s arrived in Kazakhstan, and in 2013, about forty aircraft were in service there. Interestingly the MiG-29M2 fighters put on demonstrations at air shows in Kazakhstan. This is obviously intended to spur interest in further acquisitions, as the original airframe times of the serving MiGs must be gradually nearing an end.

Malaysia

In 1995, Malaysia received sixteen single-seat and two two-seat MiG-29s valued at about 560 million US dollars. These aircraft came from the 1990 to 1998 production period, and after the fall of the Soviet Union were stored by the manufacturer as the Russian Air Force was unable to procure new aircraft. The aircraft were flown to Malaysia by An-124 transport aircraft. The goal was that the aircraft would be equipped to SD standard, however this was not achieved immediately on delivery. Instead the aircraft would be reequipped in stages. The NO-19ME radar was installed and it permitted the simultaneous engagement of two aerial targets. Interestingly, despite the aircraft's ability to employ the R-77 air-to-air missile, it was never procured by the Malaysian Air Force. The weapons load was raised and engines with an operating life of 2,000 hours were installed. The wings were modified to each carry one external fuel tank. The Malaysian Air Force requested an in-flight refueling probe that could be retrofitted. An integral refueling

probe had been included in the design of the MiG-29M and MiG-29K in the 1980s, and was mounted inside the fuselage, but adding one to the Malaysian MiG-29 was not so easily accomplished as there was simply no room left in the fuselage. A probe therefore had to be developed which could be fitted on the outside of the fuselage. One of the first version MiG-29s was converted for this purpose. The refueling probe is contained in a fairing on the left side of the fuselage and it extends for aerial refueling. The aircraft can refuel both from Russian and western tankers. The latter require only an adapter on the tanker hose. The refueling probe can be installed on any older MiG-29 with minor modifications, the job taking an hour or less. The refueling probe retrofit kit weighs a total of about 210 pounds.

The installation of a satellite communications and navigation system, TACAN, and western radio, plus ILS and IFF (Identification Friend or Foe) equipment was part of the MiG-29N. The designation MiG-29N is not an official numbering by MiG itself. Two aircraft were lost during operations and a replacement for one was purchased.

Moldavia

MiG-29s of the Soviet Fleet Air Arm of the Black Sea Fleet were stationed on Moldavian territory, and after the political upheaval they became part of the new air force. There were approximately thirty-four aircraft, the majority of them the 9.13 version (which was capable of carrying nuclear weapons). After the collapse of the Soviet Union, Moldavia was one of the poorest European countries, making it impossible for it to keep the MiG-29 in its inventory. With an area of only about 12,750 square miles, there was always the danger that the MiGs would enter foreign airspace, and there was also a serious shortage of pilots. Moldavia therefore sought someone to take the aircraft. South Yemen bought four MiGs but quickly realized that Moldavia was incapable of providing technical and logistical support and purchased no more. In 1997, a rather unexpected customer bought twenty-one MiG-29 9.13s: the USA. On closer examination, however, the purchase was not quite so unexpected. By doing so the USA on the one hand prevented hostile nations from obtaining the nuclear-capable MiG-29, while on the other it gained the opportunity to evaluate the aircraft in its own territory. What is little known is that it also purchased 500 air-to-air missiles, which might have been due to the same reasons. The total sales price is a clear indication that for Moldavia it was a

Serbian MiG-29 after overhaul by RAC MiG. *Eric Bannwarth*

Unusual camouflage scheme with shades of blue. An interesting detail here is the additional blast panel on the fuselage in front of the cannon opening. *RAC MiG*

distress sale, for according to press reports the total sum was just 81 million US dollars–less than four million dollars per aircraft.

Myanmar

The air force of Myanmar received twelve MiG-29s in 2001. Twenty more, worth 400 million US dollars, followed in 2009. This second delivery is significant, because China had previously been Myanmar's biggest supplier of weapons. China offered to sell its modern J-10 and FC-1 fighters, but they lost out to the MiG-29. Six of these aircraft were the SE variant. The MiGs are based at the Meiktila air force base near Shante.

North Korea

After India, North Korea was the second Asian country to receive the MiG-29. Once again the cause may have been the delivery of F-16s by the USA to South Korea. North Korea was the only recipient of the MiG-29 whose contract included the manufacture of spare parts. A number of aircraft were provided in half-completed condition for assembly in North Korea. This was probably done to ensure a transfer of technology. The first aircraft were assembled in 1988. It is also noteworthy that several nuclear-capable 9.13 versions were also delivered (Nos. 5 to 7), however the active jamming system was not exported to North Korea. There are approximately 30–35 examples of the MiG-29 in North Korean service.

Peru

After learning a painful lesson in the border war with Ecuador in 1995, that its obsolescent aircraft would not be able to stand up to another conflict with that country, in 1998, Peru bought sixteen single-seat (9.13) and two two-seat MiG-29s from the stocks of the White Russian Air Force. Negotiations were conducted with Russia and subsequently with White Russia, with the latter making the more favorable offer. A condition of the sale, however, was that the aircraft would have flown 30% of their airframe times. R-27 and R-73 AAMs and B-8 rocket pods were also delivered. The Peruvian Air Force's future MiG-29 pilots

underwent training in Russia from May to November 1996. The first MiG-29s arrived in the South American country one month later. When it became clear that White Russia would not be able to provide technical support and spare parts, Peru turned directly to MiG. It subsequently purchased three new MiG-29SE fighters. This type had the great advantage of having the improved NO-19ME radar, which enabled it to use the R-77 air-to-air missile. It also purchased the then new R-73 EL, which had an improved laser proximity fuse and a wide-angle seeker head. Two MiG-29s crashed during regular service, however both pilots ejected safely thanks to the excellent K-36 ejector seat.

A new contract with Russian covering the modernization of eight aircraft was signed in 2008. These aircraft were fitted with glass cockpits and the weapons system was converted for use of the R-77, Ch-31, and Ch-29. A fixed refueling probe, similar to that on the White Russian MiG-29BM, was also part of the modernization. The total airframe time was raised to 4,000 hours. The conversions were carried out in Peru by local firms, while overhaul of the engines took place in Russia.

Poland

Twelve aircraft were delivered to Poland in 1989, and the chosen pilots completed their conversion training a year earlier in the Soviet Union. After the disbandment of the Warsaw Pact, Poland strove for membership in NATO and no longer planned to buy Russian military equipment– including aircraft. Despite this, Poland unexpectedly increased its MiG-29 fleet when it exchanged eleven W-3 Sokol helicopters for the aircraft from the Czech Republic. Several of the MiG-29s encountered serious problems during the transfer flight from the Czech Republic to Poland. After deciding not to continue using the MiG-29, the Czechs had little importance to maintaining the aircraft and they were parked in the open and left to their fates. Over time moisture entered sensitive areas, and when sent to collect the aircraft Polish personnel found that they were not flyable. The Poles therefore had to remove certain parts from their MiG-29s and install them in the unserviceable Czech machines before they could be flown to Poland.

The Poles turned to Russia for the necessary spares, but the Russians allegedly demanded exorbitantly high prices for them and the Poles therefore only purchased the most vitally needed parts and carried out repairs in their own repair facilities and aviation companies. Repairs to the Czech aircraft ran to about two million US dollars per

All of these aircraft have had their weapons pylons removed for the air display. The refueling probes on the left side of the single-seaters are clearly visible. *Dr. Frikkie Bekker*

The vertical tail surfaces have received a special paint finish to mark the 53rd anniversary of the formation of the Malaysian Air Force. *Weimeng*

aircraft. This move almost doubled the number of MiG-29s in Polish service, from twelve to twenty-two. Then in 2003–04, all German MiG-29s were integrated into the Polish Air Force. The German MiG-29s were acquired for the symbolic price of 1 Euro, however the necessary maintenance and repair work cost as much as 30 million US dollars. This was still cheaper than buying new aircraft, however.

Part of the agreement obligated Poland to update its ground forces with NATO vehicles. And so Poland purchased just under 130 combat vehicles, including Leopard 2A4 tanks, though at the regular price. But back to the MiG-29. Modifications at the repair facility in Bydgoszcz saw the maximum airframe time increased to 4,000 hours and the installation of NATO-compatible radio, IFF, and navigation equipment. Polish components and a GPS set were also installed. During the entire modernization and repair operation, Poland cooperated with RSK MiG, which inspected the aircraft, delivered spare parts, and carried out final checks after all the work was done. Poland also worked with the repair facility in Baranovichi in White Russia, which maintained that country's MiG-29s. Thirty-six aircraft are in active service, seven are sources of spare parts and two are used for training at the air force school. These latter nine MiGs are former German aircraft which are time

expired or near their maximum airframe time. The MiG-29s serve in three wings, two at Minsk Mazowiecki and the third at Malbork. In 2011, the Polish government decided to modernization thirteen single-seaters and three two-seaters. For forty million US dollars, color displays, a ring laser gyroscope and satellite navigation system, a digital video camera, and new Rockwell-Collins radios were installed in cooperation with IAI of Israel. The airframe life of the original Polish MiG-29s has now been increased to 4,000 hours. The aircraft are expected to remain in service until 2030.

Peruvian Air Force MiG-29s at their home base at Chiclayo. Here again, the open air intake louvers are clearly visible. *Chris Lofting*

Here MiG-29's leading edge root extensions create clear vortices. The antenna fairings for the active ECM system on the wing tips are also clearly visible. *Chris Lofting*

Romania

Romania received its first MiG-29s, ten single-seat and two two-seat aircraft, in 1989. The pilots converted onto the MiG-29 in Kiev and then flew their aircraft home. Further deliveries raised the number of aircraft to eighteen. The Romanian Air Force lost three aircraft in crashes in 1990, and all three pilots were killed. The first accident took place during a preparation flight for an air show, when the two MiGs collided in the air. The pilot involved in the second crash was not wearing a G-suit and attempted a barrel roll at low altitude after an MAPO MiG pilot completed a similar maneuver. He probably blacked out and lost control, causing the aircraft to crash.

The year 2000 saw the birth of the Sniper Program, which was developed and offered by DASA, the aviation subsidiary of Daimler-Benz AG (now part of EADS), the Israeli company Elbit and Romanian Aerostar. The central part of the modernization was the cockpit, which was equipped with color displays and a new HUD. Also installed were an improved digital mission computer, an improved navigation system based on GPS and ring laser gyroscope,

and improved radar warning equipment. Installation of the mission computer made it possible for the aircraft to use western weapons. The first prototype made its maiden flight the same year, however poor economic conditions prevented a contract from being signed between the German and Israeli companies and the Romanian government. The company that built the MiG-29, MAPO, was not included in this program. MAPO criticized the program, stating that without the participation of the manufacturer, work on the airframe could result in an increased accident rate. All previous European non-GUS air forces have worked with MAPO when it came to modernization and especially airframe work. The Romanian MiG-29s have been in storage since 2003, as the necessary overhauls could not be carried out, rendering the aircraft non-flyable. Since joining NATO, in the long run Romania can also not avoid procuring military technology from the west, consequently there will no longer be a place for the MiG-29.

Former German Air Force MiG-29 29+18, now based at Malbork with the Polish Air Force. *RAC MiG*

Special finish in honor of Polish pilots who flew with the Allies during the Second World War. On the right inner vertical tail is the image of Marian Pisarek. *Markus Schrader*

Sudan

In 2003, the African nation of Sudan received twelve MiG-29SaE aircraft, which are similar in concept to the SMT 9.18 received by Yemen, but without the refueling probe. The sale had a total value of about 130 million US dollars, or roughly 10 million dollars per aircraft. This explains the fact that these were not new MiG-29s, rather machines that MAPO had been unable to sell after the collapse of the Soviet Union and placed in storage. In the 1990s, relations with neighboring Eritrea were extremely poor and the MiG-29 was the aircraft Sudan needed to feel armed for a possible conflict. They were later used in the Sudanese civil war. Mercenaries played a part in this war, and Libyan and Iraqi pilots flew a variety of types. The Sudan had a severe pilot shortage, especially those capable of flying the MiG-29. In 2008, a Russian flight instructor was killed in a ground attack mission against rebel positions in Khartoum. The Russians denied that the pilot had been ordered by the Defense Ministry to fly combat operations in the Sudan. This, however, led to the conclusion that foreigners were training Sudanese pilots, for it seemed rather unlikely that the Sudanese trained themselves on the MiG-29. It also seemed possible that they were former Russian Air Force pilots. This led to another secret, namely

the number of MiG-29s delivered to the Sudan. The deliveries took place at a time when Sudan was under sanctions because of its civil war. After the sanctions were softened, Russian is believed to have delivered MiG-29s by way of third countries (White Russia is often mentioned). It is thus possible that more than the twelve MiG-29s mentioned at the beginning of this chapter are in service in the Sudan, especially as the country wanted to acquire additional MiGs.

Syria

In 1987–88, Syria received about twenty MiG-29s, becoming the second export customer for the aircraft. A request for 150 examples from the Soviet Union came to nothing. Unconfirmed sources state that the MiG-29 was used as a fighter-bomber against hostile militias in the Syrian civil war that broke out in 2011. The press often reported that Syria intended to or already had procured the MiG-29M2, however nothing was heard of this in the Russian press or officially from RAC MiG. Further it became clear that in 2007, a contract had been reached for the delivery of twelve of these modified versions. When the civil war began in 2011, the Russian side held off on delivery and

Romanian MiG-29s, out of service and parked among the blast walls. *Chris Lofting*

so far there has been no official information about a later delivery. The exact number of MiG-29s on strength with the Syrian Air Force can only be estimated and may amount to 18–42 examples.

Ukraine

After the breakup of the Soviet Union the former Ukrainian Soviet Republic became an independent state. As a considerable part of the Soviet MiG-29 fleet was stationed in the former republic, from the total of about 240 examples, the Ukraine ended up with more than 150 aircraft of the 9.13 variant. Thus the Ukrainian Air Force became the second largest user of the MiG-29 worldwide. The Ukrainian pilots also suffered from low annual flying hours and it was difficult to exploit the full combat potential of the MiG-29. As well, the MiG-29s slowly neared their maximum operating time, and modernization was urgently needed if they were to continue flying. This could only be achieved with Russian help, for after all the aircraft's maker and deliverer was in that country. The present political situation is also not helpful. It is not likely that Ukraine's pro-western government will procure western military equipment and that this could mean the end of the MiG-29.

Despite this, the country formed an aerobatic team, the Ukrainian Falcons, which has performed at a number of air shows at home and abroad. The team did lose a pilot during a warm-up for an air display in France.

Because of the Ukraine's difficult economic situation, it was impossible for it to continue operating the mass of military equipment it had inherited from the Soviet Union. The country therefore tried to sell some of its MiG-29s. A number of aircraft were sold to Algeria and Azerbaijan, but in the intermediate term the country was unable to offer spares or maintenance support. At that time there were still about eighty MiG-29s in service in the Ukrainian Air Force. Since 2010, a modernization package has been worked on in the Ukraine, with participation by Russian and local companies. The aircraft's radar was improved with the addition of more modern computers, allowing its range to be increased to about sixty miles. This has enabled the fighter to use the R-77 missile. The old displays have disappeared from the cockpit, replaced by a new LCD. To date not all aircraft have been converted, however they have received a digital camouflage scheme similar to the one used by Slovakia. These updated aircraft are designated MiG-29MU1 or MUB1.

After Crimea joined Russia in 2014, some of the Ukrainian MiG-29s stationed at Belbek remained on the peninsula and were probably integrated into the Russian Air Force as required and after necessary repairs had been carried out.

Uzbekistan and Turkmenistan

Unlike in Kazakhstan, there were MiG-29 units based in Uzbekistan and Turkmenistan. And so after the collapse of the USSR the two nations acquired the MiGs located there. In 2013, there were about twenty-four aircraft in service with the Turkmenistan Air Force, and roughly thirty-nine in the Uzbekistan Air Force.

White Russia

Following the breakup of the Soviet Union, White Russia was the third largest user of MiG-29s in the CIS. The number of aircraft taken over from Soviet times varies between forty to eighty. In 1996, White Russia sold eighteen single-seat and two two-seat MiG-29s to Peru. Meanwhile the forty aircraft continued in service. Operational units were based at Bereza and Baranovichi. The state-owned aircraft maintenance facility is integrated with the latter, and in 2002, it began modernizing four aircraft, which became MiG-29BM. The MiG-29BM is a version of the 9.13 developed by White Russia in cooperation with Russian companies. This variant received the improved NO-19P radar and a new color display in the cockpit. These improvements enable it to use the RVV-AE (AA-12 Adder) and TV-guided missiles, as well as Ch-29T and Kab-500 Kr bombs and the radar-guided Ch-31P/A. A laser seeker pod has to be carried for use of laser-guided weapons. The aircraft's navigation system was also upgraded. The most obvious external change is a fixed refueling probe. Four aircraft were converted to this standard. Like the Scandinavians, the White Russian Air Force trains to use prepared sections of road, even with the Su-27. A further MiG-29 modernization program has been offered, including additional display screens, a satellite navigation system based on GPS or Glonass (Global Navigation Satellite System, a Russian satellite navigation system) and a radar that can produce ground maps. Even though this program is primarily designed for foreign users of the MiG-29, the White Russian Air Force has also shown interest.

Yemen

In 1993, Moldavia sold four MiG-29s to the recently united Yemen. Only two of these were flyable, however, and as Moldavia was incapable of providing spares or technical support Yemen had no further interest in additional MiG-29s from Moldavia. These two aircraft were, however, used in the civil war in Yemen, while the other two non-flyable machines served as sources of spare parts. Beginning in 2002, the Yemeni Air Force received about eighteen single-seat and two two-seat MiG-29s. Six aircraft were the SMT 9.18 version, which were delivered new. Later the single-seaters already in service in Yemen were brought up to the same technical standard.

Yugoslavia, Serbia

Yugoslavia became the first European country to receive the MiG-29 in 1987, when fourteen single-seaters and two two–seaters were delivered. Sheltering the aircraft proved problematic, as the existing shelters for the MiG-21 proved too small for the MiG-29. Following the breakup of Yugoslavia the MiGs were integrated into the Serbian Air Force. Approximately, two-thirds of these were destroyed on the ground during the NATO attacks in 1999, and Serbia simply could not compete with NATO's numerical superiority. The Serbians reacted quickly, however; for example they analyzed how the Allies proceeded against Iraq during the First Gulf War. The latter had thrown its entire military against the enemy, but its forces were far inferior and Iraq lost a great deal of war materiel. Conscious of NATO's superiority, Serbia was determined not to repeat this mistake and to provoke as few further losses as possible. The Serbs achieved a military success in shooting down an American F-117 stealth fighter. To this date there is still uncertainty as to whether the American aircraft was shot down by a surface-to-air missile, ground fire, or a Serbian aircraft.

In fact, however, the Serbians were subsequently unable to maintain regular flight operations and their MiG-29s were in increasingly urgent need of repairs and spare parts. Negotiations were carried out with White Russia, however no contract was concluded. Serbia's remaining five MiGs underwent a thorough overhaul by RAC MiG valued at 10 million US dollars. Today they are stationed at Batajnica with the 101st Fighter Wing.

Overhauled MiG-29 9.13 of the Ukrainian Air Force armed with R-73 AAMs. This aircraft also has the extended blast shield around the cannon muzzle. *Chris Lofting*

MiG-29UB in front of a closed aircraft shelter. *Theo van Vliet*

The ramp at Ivano Air Base with modernized MiG-29U1 and MUB1 aircraft. *Theo van Vliet*

Ukraine is the second country to use a digital camouflage scheme for its aircraft. The scheme seen here is made up of four colors. *Theo van Vliet*

The trident emblem on the vertical tail is actually a stylized diving bird of prey. *Chris Lofting*

MiG-29 in a special paint scheme for the seventieth anniversary of the Hungarian Air Force in 2008. *RAC MiG*

Image of an Italian-made Caproni-Reggiane Re.2000, a type flown by the Hungarian Air Force during the Second World War, on the upper surfaces of a MiG-29.

MiG-29BM with retrofitted refueling probe.

This camouflage scheme was intended to make the aircraft difficult to see against a earth-colored background or provide concealment on the ground when away from paved surfaces. As may be seen here, it was rather less effective at higher altitudes. *Dr. Stefan Petersen*

Chapter 4
The German MiGs

From the NVA
to the Bundeswehr

The first rumors about procurement of the MiG-29 by East Germany were heard in 1984, when then defense minister Armeegeneral Heinz Hoffmann told a Swedish colleague this during a visit to the fighter wing at Peenemünde. Between March 1988 and May 1989, the GDR (East Germany) received twenty single-seat and four two-seat MiG-29s worth one-billion East German marks and was thus the first nation of the Warsaw Pact to receive the type. The single-seat versions were the Type 9.12A, which had a slightly less capable radar than the 9.12 version used by the USSR. This radar lacked the free search feature.

The new aircraft were assigned to Jagdgeschwader 3 "Vladimir Komarov" (a Soviet cosmonaut killed during testing of the first Soyuz space capsule in 1967) at Preschen (near Cottbus), close to the Polish border. Pilot conversion took place in the Soviet Union in 1987. Flying operations from Preschen involved cooperation with the Polish Air Force, as the approach to land often meant that the German MiGs had to enter Polish airspace, due to the proximity of their airfield to the Polish border. An agreement was reached between East Germany and Poland concerning these airspace incursions, as Polish aircraft also had to enter German airspace to land at their bases at Sczecin and Jelina Gora. A flight simulator was acquired for pilot training, but as there was as yet no suitable building at Preschen, training had to be carried out in a cockpit mockup.

The first squadron at Preschen became operational in May 1988. The single-seat MiGs wore a three-color upper camouflage scheme consisting of shades of brown and green. This was effective when the aircraft was on

This UB also wears a green-brown camouflage scheme. Other UBs flown by the East German Air Force wore a two-tone grey scheme. *Rob Schleiffert*

MiG-29UB during engine start. Wearing a sound protection helmet, the ground crewman was in contact with the pilot by cable and throat microphone. *Rob Schleiffert*

Back from a sortie—the refueling truck is standing by, the technicians begin reading the flight recorder data. The blue letter Q beneath the glazing is an indication that the machine has a very good maintenance standard. *Rob Schleiffert*

The yellow markings beneath the cockpit glazing mark the emergency canopy releases. The small parachute behind the braking chute is the extraction chute, which pulled the main chute from its compartment. *Rob Schleiffert*

75

the ground and was also intended to provide concealment from higher-flying enemy aircraft. Curiously, some of the two-seaters wore a scheme of two shades of grey optimized for air combat. German reunification officially took place on October 3, 1990, and the Federal German Air Force took possession of all of the assets of the East German Air Force, including its MiG-29s. While it soon became obvious that the other types (MiG 21, MiG-23, and SU-17M4) would not remain in service (although they underwent extensive testing by the Technical Airworthiness Center for Aircraft [WTD] and had some surprises in store for NATO), the MiG-29 was thoroughly evaluated to determine if it could serve as an interim solution pending introduction of the Eurofighter. Of course there were differences of opinion, which may have had an ideological background. After all−a Soviet fighter in the Federal German Air Force?

As there was much about the MiG-29 that was still unknown in the west at that time and it was thought to probably be equal to western fighters (in the opinion of the German Air Force), the opportunity to thoroughly test the most modern Russian frontline fighter was exploited. In October 1990, two single-seaters and two two-seaters were flown to Manching for trials with WTD 61. Additional

tests using four MiG-29s were carried out simultaneously at Wittmund and these were continued on Sardinia in April and May. In early 1991, *Jagdgeschwader 3* at Preschen became Erprobungsgeschwader MiG-29 (MiG 29 Test Wing), part of the 5th Luftwaffe Division. When the trials were completed, the Luftwaffe decided to employ the MiG-29 in the air defense role. Deciding factors may have been the type's outstanding maneuverability combined with the highly agile R-73 (AA-11 Archer) air-to-air missile and the simple but extremely effective helmet sight. In simulated combat against the F-16 the MiG-29 proved superior, and the MiG-29's radar proved much more resistant to ECM then the testers in Bavaria had expected. The opportunity for German MiG-29 pilots to gain experience in air combat maneuvers with NATO fighters and develop new tactics, which would never have been possible with the Phantom, must have factored into the thinking. The experience gained with the MiG-29 must surely have been taken into account during the service introduction of the Eurofighter.

During the run-up to the first Iraq war, the Allied air forces were extremely interested in obtaining information about the MiGs from Germany. Once again

Aircraft 679 of the East German Air Force would become 29+12 in service with the Bundesluftwaffe. Close examination of the photo reveals that the pilot is wearing the old 3Sh-5A helmet, not the 3Sh-7A developed for the MiG-29 and Su-27. The newer helmet was not procured by East Germany. *Dr. Stefan Petersen*

Here the future 29+12 clearly displays its grey undersurfaces, which from the ground concealed the aircraft against the sky. *Dr. Stefan Petersen*

The new code of the Bundesluftwaffe has already been painted on this aircraft's starboard air intake, while the old NVA code 604 is still present on the tip of its vertical tail. The last MiG-29 flight in NVA markings took place on September 26, 1990, the first flight in Bundesluftwaffe markings on October 19, 1990. *Rob Schleiffert*

NVA MiG-29s 668 and 604, which in Federal German service became 29+01 and 29+07. At this altitude the camouflage scheme shows its effectiveness against a land background. *Dr. Stefan Petersen*

This photo makes it very clear that the NVA's brown-green camouflage scheme was designed for use at lower altitudes. *Dr. Stefan Petersen*

Once again the upper surface camouflage is ineffective against a cloudless sky. *Dr. Stefan Petersen*

the type's radar caused the experts to sit up and take notice. Its performance had been seriously underestimated, and thus during simulated combats the pilots of the F-15s and F-16s were surprised to learn by radio that they had been shot down beyond visual range (BVR) without ever having got the MiGs in their sights. This is most likely a mixture of fact and legend, for years later the Germans had a difficult time with the MiG-29 radar against F-15s, F-16s, and F-18s. The fact is, however, that the MiG-29's radar originated in the 1970s, while the radars in the American fighters in the 1990s were improved versions of the original systems, making it impossible to draw an objective comparison. In any case the trials with the MiG-29 at Manching shattered illusions about "antiquated Russian electronics" (although this was partly justified in some fields). Concerning this, at the Paris Air Show in 1998 a representative of the Antonov Design Bureau stated that they (the Russians) were basically satisfied with the functionality of the Soviet electronics but not with the size of the equipment.

After the trials at Manching, NATO had the ability to develop technical and tactical countermeasures before they took on the moderately trained and outnumbered Iraqis. Germany loaned a MiG-29 (29+06) to the USA, where it underwent extensive testing. It was later returned to the Luftwaffe. Following the conclusion of testing at Wittmund, Sardinia, and Manching, beginning in 1993, the MiG-29s were moved from Preschen to Laage (near Rostock) in Mecklenburg–Western Pomerania. The move was completed in 1994. There they formed the *1. Jagdstaffel* (1st Fighter Squadron), while the F-4 Phantoms stationed there formed the *2. Jagdstaffel*. The MiGs' role there was to defend the airspace over northeastern Germany. During its period of operations it proved advantageous to use the two types together in the air defense role. For the German F-4s had been fitted with the modern radar (APG-65) from the F-18, together with the AMRAAM air-to-air missile. The Phantom was thus better able to locate and engage distant targets, while the MiG-29 assumed the close combat role. For use of the MiG-29 by the Luftwaffe and within NATO, in cooperation with the manufacturer Mikoyan, components were converted so that NATO-compatible radio, navigation, and IFF systems could be used. Cockpit placards and instruments were switched to English and anti-collision lights were installed. The company MAPS was founded after the breakup of the USSR, and it included Mikoyan and DASA. The latter later became part of EADS. Strangely the laser, the part of the IRST that provided range measurement for the cannon, was deactivated. The reason

given was protection of the pilots' eyesight from the powerful laser, however the laser was activated during several exercises.

The components installed for the Russian RSBN navigation system were replaced by TACAN, its western equivalent. While the RSBN was more accurate, the Germans did not want to use two different systems, and as TACAN was already in use in other aircraft, the ground components of the RSBN and those in the MiG-29 had to go. The Soviet identification friend or foe system also had to be replaced. With the Soviet system, the N-019 automatically transmitted a coded signal to the airborne object with radar contact. Based on the response from the object, it was graded friendly, neutral, or hostile and displayed on the HUD. Conversion to NATO standard equipment also eliminated the ability to data link to ground control. Soviet doctrine envisaged the MiG-29 being guided to the target from the ground by radar. The MiG-29 received coded signals from the ground, and the course, speed, and altitude of the target to be intercepted were displayed in the cockpit. The pilot received optical and acoustic signals. The advantage of this was that the MiG-29s in the air did not need to switch on their onboard radars and thus their radars did not betray their positions. If the data feed from the ground was severed or jammed by the enemy, the MiG's radar automatically switched on and went to target search/pursuit mode.

Another innovation of the German MiGs was replacement of the original target camera with a video camera with which to record simulated combats. This made it easier to evaluate the engagements. In 1998, Michael Waldenberg, general designer of the MiG-29, declared that the German pilots were flying the MiG-29 in the style for which he and his compatriots had developed it. It was they who got the most out of the MiG-29, which was reflected in the highest dynamic airframe loads of any MiG-29 fleet in the world. This style of flying took its toll, however, and cracks were soon discovered at the roots of the tail fins caused by the high loads produced by the exhausting style in which the MiGs were being flown. The maker MAPO MiG sent technicians to Laage and they applied reinforcements in the affected areas, restoring full operational capability.

In 2002, it was leaked by the press that all of the German MiGs would be handed over to Poland in 2004. In July 2003, the Defense Minister Peter Struck signed an agreement with Poland, transferring the MiGs to Poland for the symbolic price of one Euro. Delivery began in September of that year and was completed in August 2004. The MiGs' new base was Bydgoszcz. An official

The MiG peeling away from the photographer carries R-27 simulators and R-73 missiles. *Dr. Stefan Petersen*

Aircraft 29+18 ready for take off from Laage. Note the badge of *JG 73* on the vertical stabilizer. *Stefan Gawlista*

In Bundesluftwaffe service the camouflage scheme was changed to air superiority grey, as the MiG-29's role took place at high altitudes, making the earth camouflage on the upper surfaces redundant. *Dr. Stefan Petersen*

Aircraft 29+01
with simulated
full armament
load for aerial
combat. *Dr.
Stefan Petersen*

ceremony was held at Laage to mark the MiGs' departure. Many military and civilian personnel were sad to see the MiGs go, for it had been an exciting time for all. Altogether the MiG-29 logged about 33,000 hours in German service (about 6,000 of these with the NVA), equivalent to about 1,400 hours per aircraft. They will always be fondly remembered by many former comrades in arms, including myself.

Air Combat Exercises

Laage frequently received visitors from foreign air forces who came to fly against the MiG-29. The types involved included the Mirage 2000 and F1, Sepecat Jaguar, Super Etendard, AMX, Harrier, Tornado, Su-22, F-4 Phantom, F-15, F-16, F-18, A-10, and the Gripen.

Nations which sent pilots included the USA, France, Sweden, Denmark, Switzerland, Belgium, Finland, Hungary, Poland (these last two brought their own MiG-29s), Turkey, the Netherlands, Great Britain, and Italy.

Aircraft 29+10 was painted in this special finish for the last deployment to the USA. The design was created by one of the wing's civilian employees. *Stefan Gawlista*

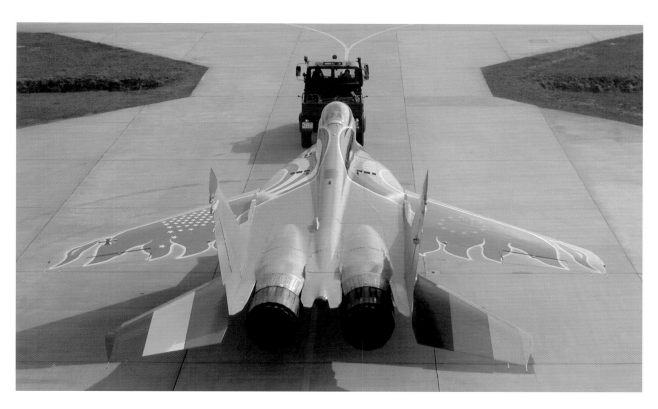

Here the special scheme can be seen in all its glory. *Stefan Gawlista*

MiG-29s with American F-15Es from Lakenheath, Great Britain. *Peter Steiniger*

Foreign Exercises with the MiG-29

Europe

The German MiG-29 pilots also often had the opportunity to demonstrate their skills outside Germany. This took place primarily in Sardinia, where the NATO countries regularly held intensive air combat exercises among themselves and with allied nations. Part of the reason for these exercises was to develop and perfect air combat tactics for other NATO types and other allies to use against the MiG-29, for the USA and NATO increasingly expected encounters with hostile MiG-29s during wars against so-called "rogue states."

These air battles may also have given new impetus to air combat tactics in general and the development of new combat aircraft. On the other hand the tactics employed by the MiGs constantly underwent further development, including BVR (Beyond Visual Range) combat. In view of the growing obsolescence of the MiG's radar, this had to be part of the exercises.

Over the years, the MiG-29's demonstrated abilities in close combat undoubtedly had a major impact on the direction of tactics for the Eurofighter, then still in testing, for the MiG-29 was by far the most agile type in service with the Luftwaffe. Not every foreign exercise in which the MiGs took part will be described in the following text, only those that represented a high point or otherwise stood out.

1991 was the first year in which real air combat exercises took place. The results must have helped convince the Luftwaffe to find further use for this type, which was almost unbeatable in close-in combat. These detachments took place annually from 1993 to 1999, and for the last time in 2003. In 1993, *Jagdgeschwader 73* took the international stage for the first time at NATO air combat exercises. The competition had already been warned, for the MiG-29 had already spent time being tested in Sardinia and had flown against the entire range of NATO combat aircraft. The outstanding capabilities of the Soviet design came as a shock to the western side. In 1997, the MiG again demonstrated its capabilities. The engines were switched from "training regime" (see the chapter on engines) to "war regime RPT" after which the MiG-29 successfully intercepted a U-2.

In 1996, the MiGs visited Spain, where they conducted exercises with Spanish F-18s. That same year, and in 1998, the Fulcrums participated in the TLP (Technical Leadership Program) at Florennes, Belgium. There they were flown against all of the fighter types flown by the European NATO partners, in some cases with convincing victories for the MiGs. During one detachment it was heard that during a close-in engagement with F-16s they had scored several simulated victories against the MiGs, but only after taking eighteen simulated R-73 hits themselves. Of course no MiG can carry eighteen R-73 missiles, but as the F-16s were taken out so quickly, it was decided not to take the F-16s out of the exercise after they were shot down, but instead to immediately send them into another engagement.

In 2002, the MiG-29s visited Switzerland for the first time, at Dübendorf airfield. After familiarization flights for the mountain scenario, both close-in and BVR combats were carried out. During the first flights the Swiss underestimated the capabilities of the twenty-five-year-old MiGs, especially their agility at low speeds, and suffered defeats. But now and then the MiGs also failed to score hits because of the high cockpit workload in combat and the associated looking away from the HUD, which meant that the pilots could not always keep the target in sight. After their initial defeat by the MiGs, the Swiss took them more seriously and exploited their advantages in BVR combat. In 2003, the Swiss in turn visited Laage. The last detachment for the German MiGs was in September 2003, on Sardinia and this represented another high point, for Israeli combat aircraft (F-15I) took part in a NATO exercise in Europe for the first time. Engagements were flown in visual and beyond visual ranges. Both the Germans and the Israelis spoke very positively about this exercise, which proved very valuable and informative for both sides.

In the USA

The Americans were also very eager to compete against the MiG-29 on their home soil, but the type's short range and inability to refuel in the air initially ruled out a flight to the USA. While the German MiGs could carry an external tank under the fuselage, this was not sufficient. The Russian MiG-29S could also carry two external fuel tanks under the wings, which while inadequate for a nonstop flight across the Atlantic, was sufficient for a crossing with stops en route. And so seven German MiG-29s were modified to carry two underwing tanks in addition to the fuselage tank (see fuel system). This "island hopping" method envisaged a departure from Laage followed by flights to Scotland, Iceland, Greenland, Canada, and the USA (the latter two countries in several stages).

A GPS system was also installed in the aircraft, as the TACAN was not suitable for such long distances.

And so in 1999, the MiG-29s landed in North America for the first time. The MiGs caused a sensation wherever they went, for it was an opportunity to see one of the main threats of the former Soviet Union up close and at home. Their destination was Nellis Air Force Base near Las Vegas, where they took part in Exercise Red Flag. The MiGs went to Nellis three more times, not as participants in Red Flag but as special guests to train with and test the locally based units. After all Nellis was a base where new weapons and tactics were tested.

Climatic conditions were twofold. On the one hand cloud or other visual obstructions were not common, which was ideal for flying activities. On the other hand the heat on the ground was extreme, as the base is located at the edge of the very hot Mojave Desert. German engine mechanics measured the air temperature in the shade (of which there was very little) before en engine test run and found it to be 125 degrees Fahrenheit!

With appropriate guidelines or no impositions of restrictions, the MiGs were able to exploit their strengths, only in close-in combat, but this was known from the outset. The MiGs did, however, earn new respect from the American pilots. And the German ground personnel were also no slouches—when technical problems arose, they worked

until they were rectified, which could mean several hours of work under a blazing sun.

In conclusion, the MiG proved itself in the extreme temperatures, even though some systems would have had to have been adjusted if the MiGs operated in such regions long term (although temperatures almost as high prevailed in the central Asian military districts of the former USSR).

The MiGs went to Nellis for the last time in 2002. During the first part of the exercise the MiGs flew against F-15s, F-16s, A-10s, and F/A-18s, with no restrictions or advantages bestowed on any of the parties. This was a sobering experience, especially for the Americans—once again especially in close-in combat. In the second part of the exercise the MiGs flew in the aggressor role and the Americans used their advanced airborne radars and long-range missiles, which was much more disadvantageous for the MiGs. This was supposed to serve as training for the Americans in how to deal with the MiG-29 without getting into close-in combat, where they had a poorer hand. Several selected American pilots took part in the exercise, among the best of their fraternity, in order to then disseminate their knowledge throughout the air force.

Immediately after Red Flag the MiGs went to Key West, Florida, for Exercise Agile Archer. The exercise was hosted

German MiG-29 after modification to carry 300-gallon external fuel tanks beneath the wings.

German
MiG-29s on the
ramp at Nellis
AFB, Nevada.

MiGs in a
maintenance
hangar at Nellis.

Ready for an
engine test run
at Nellis.

A German Air Force MiG-29 over the vast
Canadian boreal forest. *Peter Steiniger*

On the ramp at CFB Cold Lake in Alberta, Canada for Exercise Maple Flag 2000.

by the Florida Air National Guard from Jacksonville. The Key West area offered a better environment for aerial combat, so the exercise was held there. For the National Guard this meant a cost sharing arrangement, in which the Navy, as the home team, used the time in Key West to allow some of its aircraft and pilots to take part in the exercise, including the famous Top Gun squadron. The Naval Strike and Air Warfare Center is located at Key West. The usual opponents were joined by F-14s and F-5s, with the latter proving a tough opponent for the MiGs. BVR scenarios were also flown, giving the navy pilots the chance to become familiar with the characteristics of the N-019, for example its acquisition range and how to correctly interpret the indications from their radar warning receivers when illuminated by the N-019. This enabled them to develop appropriate countermeasures and suitable tactics. In contrast to earlier exercises in North America, at Key West the MiG-29s were able to exploit their advantages unrestricted, something the navy in particular wanted. Even if they received a few bloody noses, from the point of view of the navy pilots, and indeed the German pilots, it was a great opportunity to learn and practice something new. An American navy pilot got to the heart of it: a MiG-29 in the hands of a German pilot was the most dangerous opponent

a combat pilot could meet in close combat and if they could defeat a MiG there in Key West they could do it anywhere in the world.

During one of the last-named detachments in 2002, a new type of pressure suit was tested with the MiG-29. In a normal pressure suite pressurized air from the aircraft systems is pumped into chambers and pockets in the suit to force blood back into the core and head under high g-forces. But as air is compressible and has to be constantly repressurized, important moments are lost during which the pilot has to carry out special muscle tensioning techniques. In developing a new suit a Swiss company used the dragonfly as its inspiration, which is how the suit got its name. Liquid chambers are integrated into the suit and these maintain the same pressure on the body as the g-forces prevailing at the moment. And as water is not compressible and is already against the body, the appropriate counter-pressure is exerted as g-forces increase. The suit also no longer has to be connected via fittings in the cockpit to the aircraft's pressure system, as the medium is part of the suit. This suit is now also used by German Eurofighter pilots. The suit originally contained several quarts of fluid, however this was later reduced to a fraction of the original quantity.

2003 was the last year the MiGs flew from Laage to America. Their destination this time was Eglin Air Force Base. The high point of this deployment was the opportunity for the MiG-29s to fire their R-27 and R-73 air-to-air missiles at F-4 Phantom drones. These firings were carried out with the Eurofighter in mind, for valuable experience was gained by live firings of the R-73, the most agile short-range AAM in the world. The Dragonfly suit was also extensively tested at Eglin, with an eye to its future use in the Eurofighter. The engines' RPT regime was again activated and gave the pilots enormous power reserves in air combat.

In 2000, the MiGs flew from Laage to CFB Cold Lake, in the Canadian province of Alberta for the first time. There the MiG-29s trained with the Canadian and American air forces and other NATO partners using the base's huge training areas. Because of its enormous size and large unpopulated areas, Canada offered outstanding conditions. In places there were as many as several dozen aircraft in the air at the same time, although not all were involved in the exercise scenarios. There, too, the MiGs flew in the aggressor role.

The Canadians were the first to introduce a new optical trick on fighter aircraft: they painted a false canopy on the undersides of their CF-18s. This was supposed to confuse an opponent, because with a quick glance it was impossible for him to tell if he was looking at the top or bottom of the CF-18 and therefore could not tell the aircraft's exact attitude. This might cause him to initiate a wrong maneuver. This subsequently inspired a number of air forces to apply this fake cockpit to their own aircraft, including the German MiGs.

The End of the German MiGs

At the beginning of 2002, an agreement was reached between Germany and Poland covering the transfer of the German MiG-29s to Poland. The main reason was the coming introduction into service of the Eurofighter in 2004, which was also the year that the MiG-29s would leave service. As the MiGs had logged many flying hours, which would have made necessary a thorough overhaul, by handing the aircraft over to the Poles the Germans rid themselves of this expensive procedure. This was understandable economically, for the introduction of the Eurofighter had run into delays and the country was paying even though it did not have the aircraft. The first MiGs flew to their new base at Bydgoszcz, Poland, in September 2003. The era of the German MiG-29 ended on August 4, 2004, when the last MiGs left German soil. As already stated,

many aircraft were time expired and in their new Polish home they would receive a thorough overhaul. These revealed cracks in the structure, the wing and tail fin roots. Russian specialists stated that the German MiGs on average had 1,300 flying hours on them, but because of the "demanding" way they had been flown by German pilots this was equivalent to 2,500 hours.

In Poland, the MiGs were immediately converted to NATO standards. After the thorough overhaul and NATO conversion, the MiGs were based at Malbork and the MiG-21s there were retired. When looked at dispassionately, it is obvious that, even with serious modifications, the MiG-29 could not replace the Eurofighter. But it is certainly also true that western industry has its own interests in this regard. This is absolutely normal if one has or can create the conditions in which to develop and produce one's own aircraft. The best examples of this are Sweden and France, which for decades have been meeting their requirements for combat aircraft with domestic products. The creation of jobs and new technologies was out of the question. Because of the confusion and the collapse of many companies, during the early and mid-1990s, the Russian armaments industry was likely incapable of offering the large-scale and reliable production of a modernization MiG-29 (in this case the MiG-29M tested in 1986). The technical components of the then MiG-29M (which later became the MiG-29SMT in the 1990s) were not likely the reason why the MiG-29 was not selected for the Luftwaffe, for this version was on a modern level. The manufacturer MiG would also certainly have been in a position to provide the aircraft, but many and important subcontractors had gone under during this period. As the Russian Air Force was not ordering any MiG-29s because of its restricted budget, the MiG production lines were almost at a standstill. A few sales to Asia were not enough to provide a financial cushion with which to purchase new production aircraft and improve the pay of the employees. Many young people saw no future in the poorly paid Russian armaments industry. The way was thus blocked for the modern and reliable construction of the latest MiG-29.

In conclusion it must also be said that the MiG-29's radar technology in particular and its limited fuel capacity were also reasons why the Bundesluftwaffe could not consider the MiG-29 as a full value fighter aircraft for the twenty-first century. The radar did not provide enough tactical displays and the workload in the cockpit was very high. It was almost impossible to display individual aircraft from a formation and it was only possible to attack the leading aircraft. The R-27 was comparable with the AIM-7 Sparrow, but it had long since been replaced by the AIM-

120 AMRAAM, which was superior to the R-27 (as it had Fire and Forget capability and much greater range). The NATO TACAN system with which the MiG-29 had been reequipped was more imprecise than a really precise navigation aid. The LA-ZUR data link system had been disabled when the MiGs were inherited from the NVA, to say nothing of the decommissioning of the laser range finder. All of this made it almost impossible for the German MiG-29s to effectively engage modern opponents beyond visual range. It was and is, however, a perfect close-in dogfighter–but that was not enough for the Luftwaffe.

And then there was the fuel problem. The MiG-29 had been created in the doctrine of the late 1960s, and its primary purpose had been to defend the USSR against lone intruders, with a secondary role of providing air cover for the ground forces. Unlike the Su-27, it had not been designed for long patrols, therefore it had been designed with a smaller fuel capacity. The Bundesluftwaffe nurtured a different doctrine, favoring aircraft which had a significantly greater range and, especially after the collapse of the Warsaw Pact, loiter time in the target area.

In any case, even though India is bringing its aircraft up to a more modern standard, the MiG-29's future is foreseeable, for there will likely be few further large-scale MiG-29 programs anywhere in the world. In the MiG's homeland, there are further delays in the introduction of the most modern versions of the MiG-29, which have been going on for a long time. The fact is that the MiG-29 was a path-breaking aircraft that served as the measuring stick for designers worldwide.

In 2013, all flying units of the German Armed Forces were renamed, and *JG 73 "Steinhoff"* became *Taktisches Luftwaffengeschwader 73 "Steinhoff"* (Tactical Air Force Wing 73).

Aircraft were moved about the airfield by tow vehicles. An additional tow bar was used to back the MiGs into hangars or aircraft shelters. *Stefan Gawlista*

Maintenance

 JG 73 initially had two large maintenance hangars, with one hangar primarily dedicated to work in the mechanical area and one in the field of electronics. These hangars were equipped with extensive ground equipment and tool kits and roof cranes were also installed. Just about any job covered by an agreement with the Russian service center could be carried out in these hangars. Because of a lack of equipment, however, some welding work could not be done by the *Geschwader* at Cottbus, and some other repairs were carried out at the repair facility in Manching. There was never a case, however, in which a German MiG-29 had to be completely disassembled and sent back to Russia. On the other hand, on occasion Russian specialists came and worked on the aircraft at *JG 73*'s base. The work was done in a two-layer system in which military and civilian personnel worked on the aircraft together. As well, sometimes work had to be carried out on a weekend, when certain aircraft

had to be available at the start of the week or a certain number of serviceable MiGs had to be available. One can say that each system had its own specialist group with personnel responsible for that technology.

There were two former aircraft shelters that were usable for a variety of repairs, for example to fuel and hydraulic systems, engine and gearbox changes, work on radars, and much more. A total of eighteen aircraft could be accommodated in the hangars and the two shelters.

Technical personnel were trained on the MiG within the unit and were instructed by *Geschwader* personnel. In very specialized subjects the personnel were trained by factory personnel from Russia within the *Geschwader*.

B10/B11 maintenance shelter. Among other things, these were used for special work on the aircraft's radar, but also for airframe or engine work.

RAUCHEN VERBOTEN

The Elo hangar was used mainly for work on electrical/electronic systems. If space was short in the maintenance hangar, work on mechanical components was also carried out in the Elo hangar. On the right in the photo is an F-4F Phantom.

Aircraft Shelters

The devastating low-level attacks against Arab airfields by the Israeli Air Force during the Six Day War in 1967, demonstrated the vulnerability of combat aircraft parked in rows on airfields. The result, in the east and west, was the construction of hardened aircraft shelters. The following is a description of the design philosophy and operating modes of Soviet shelters in particular. These were constructed on every airfield for individual fighters or fighter-bombers up to a certain size. The aircraft housed in them were protected against bombs falling nearby and resulting fragments. The aircraft were not simply housed there, rather their engines were started and pre-takeoff preparations were made inside the shelters. In the event of war they would also have been armed there. The shelters also provided a certain degree of protection against gunfire from attacking aircraft or direct hits by small-caliber bombs. In the Iraq War of 1991, however, it was shown that there were suitable bombs available which could destroy the shelter and the aircraft inside with direct hits. The point of such structures remains questionable in a time of long-range precision-guided weapons and heavy air defenses,

but apart from direct hits, these shelters provide good protection against fragments. Packed with electronics, modern aircraft can be rendered unserviceable by minor damage.

The shelter also protects the aircraft against the weather. Ground personnel and pilots can work on the aircraft in dry conditions. The ground personnel carry out maintenance and repairs directly on the aircraft inside the shelter, topping off fluids, replacing tires or brakes, positioning drip trays, and carrying out other maintenance tasks. The advantage of this is that the aircraft does not need to be taken to a hangar each time, which in an emergency saves time and avoids concentrating the aircraft in one place, for if a hangar is hit several aircraft can be destroyed at once. Connections for several types of fluids are present inside the shelters and a few even have ammunition storage, some near and some in the shelter.

Concrete sections are assembled to construct a shelter. The shape is roughly semicircular, with the front and rear vertical. The latter has an exhaust channel that vents the large exhaust stream from the shelter when the aircraft's engines are started. The front of the shelter has two massive steel-reinforced concrete doors that move on rails and seal the shelter. The doors are usually opened by electric motors.

A typical shelter with opened sliding doors.

If these are put out of action, a lever is pulled which releases a locking mechanism. Gravity then opens the doors, as the rails are installed on a slight downward incline. Grass and in some cases small trees are planted on the roof of the shelter to improve camouflage. As the airfield can undoubtedly be identified as such from the air, false taxiways are also laid down, with no shelters at their end. Of course these shelters exist in different sizes, depending on the aircraft they are intended to accommodate. The East German Air Force shelters at Laage airfield near Rostock were originally created for the Su-22 fighter-bomber. When these were retired by the Bundeswehr, the shelters were then used to accommodate MiG-29s.

Emergency Arrestor Gear ("MiG Catcher")

The "MiG Catcher," as it was known in the parlance of the East German Air Force, was a proven safety system. It was developed in Dresden in the late 1970s, and tested at Alteno airfield. The airfield was not only used by MiGs but by aircraft from other manufacturers as well. If an aircraft encountered problems while on approach or during landing, a large net was strung across the end of the runway, extending across its entire width. This system was of course also used during aborted takeoffs. Above a certain speed, of course, even this system could not prevent an accident. In general it could arrest an aircraft weighing up to twenty-two tons at a maximum speed of 225 miles per hour in 1,080 feet. With the transfer of the MiG-29s from Preschen to Laage, a mobile arrestor was brought there and remained in use until 2004.

A "MiG Catcher" on display at the museum in Finow with a MiG-23MF.

Übersicht der Bordnummern

NVA-Kennung	Bundeswehr-Kennung	Polen-Kennung
604	29+01	4116
607	29+02	Ersatzteilspender
615	29+03 (Exponat BW-Museum Berlin-Gatow)	-
628	29+04	4111
635	29+05	4118
661	29+06	Ersatzteilspender
668	29+07	4101
669	29+08	Trainingsmodell
670	29+09 (Absturz)	-
676	29+10	Trainingsmodell
677	29+11	Ersatzteilspender
679	29+12	4113
684	29+14	Ersatzteilspender
693	29+15	Ersatzteilspender
699	29+16	4103
745	29+17	4104
777	29+18	4120
778	29+19	Ersatzteilspender
785	29+20	4121
786	29+21	4122
148 (UB)	29+22	4110
179 (UB)	29+23	4115
181 (UB)	29+24	4105
185 (UB)	29+25	4123

MiG-29 9.13 of the Peruvian 6th Air Group at Chiclayo. Note the antenna fairings for the ECM system on the wing tips. *Chris Lofting*

Chapter 5
MiG-29 Variants

MiG-29 9.13

It soon became obvious that the fuel capacity of the first version of the MiG-29 (9.12) was inadequate to give the type a satisfactory range, and consideration was given as to how to overcome this shortcoming. As the MiG-29M was already being planned, no dramatic measures were taken to produce the 9.13. By dispensing with a redesign of the upper air intakes the designers did not have much scope to increase fuel capacity. Fuselage internal tank Number 1 was enlarged, allowing about 440 pounds of additional fuel to be carried. Other changes affected the two inboard underwing hardpoints. These were connected to the fuel system, so that in addition to the 400-gallon centerline tank, two 300-gallon underwing tanks could also be carried. As a result, ferry range was increased to about 1,800 miles.

It had long been clear that a simple chaff-flare system to interfere with AAM guidance systems would no longer be adequate against the future airborne radars of the new generation of American fighters. Now the radar itself would have to be jammed. The first MiG-29 variant, the 6.12, had a radar warning device but no active jammer. And so the Gardeniya-1FU ECM system was installed, which acted as an active radar jammer and provided 360° coverage. The system was also installed in the MiG-29M. The associated avionics of the jammer transmitter and the larger fuel tank were the cause for the dorsal hump, which is the trademark of this machine and resulted in it being named Fatback, even though this hump is even larger on the MiG-29SMT. The first three aircraft were converted from MiG-29 9.12s in 1983 and testing began in 1984, with more than 400 test flights completed. Production totaled 400 aircraft and ran from 1986–91. Interestingly the first fighter units to equip with the new MiG-29 9.13 were not based in the Soviet

Union, rather they were Soviet units of the 16th Air Army in East Germany. This is a reflection of the very tense ratio of forces that existed with NATO at that time.

MiG-29S 9.13S

When the new R-77 air-to-air missile with active radar homing became available, there was obviously a desire to use it with the MiG-29, and so the radar carried by the MiG-29 9.13 was upgraded. The improved set with the designation N-019M Topas could be used with the new air-to-air missile, and two targets could be engaged simultaneously instead of the previous one. The radar's resistance to jamming was also further improved. Other changes affected the flight control system. The maximum allowable angle of attack increased by two degrees to 28 degrees. Weapons load was increased by 1,985 pounds to 7,050 pounds. Since 1991 the 9.12 and 9.13 variants of the MiG-29 in service with the Russian Air Force have been brought up to MiG-29S standard, as financing for the more modern MiG-29M did not materialize.

MiG-29SD 9.12SD

This variant is a mixture of the first MiG-29 9.12 and the MiG-29S 9.13. In 1994, the Malaysian Air Force decided to purchase fourteen single-seaters and two two-seaters, however they insisted on an air refueling probe for the single-seat aircraft. And so MiG had to develop a refueling probe that did not result in high costs and could simply be retrofitted to existing aircraft. Use of the refueling probe from the MiG-29K, which was fully retractable, was not practical for space reasons and excessive modification costs. As a result, a probe that could be mounted on the exterior of the aircraft was developed, similar to that of the Tornado GR.1. MiG drew on the experience gained in trials with the MiG-25 and MiG-31 production aircraft. In 1995, Roman Taskayev completed the first aerial refueling by a MiG-29 with this special probe from an IL-78 tanker. The aircraft was later given the Bort number 357 and was displayed at several air shows.

The special assembly weighed 143 pounds and the additional fittings and piping weighed 66 pounds. The probe could be installed or removed in an hour (provided that the factory had made the necessary modification). The probe was retractable and could be fitted to all 9.12 and 9.13 variants. Ultimately, this special refueling probe was used for the SMT program.

The MiG-29SD did not have the larger internal fuselage tank, but to increase range two underwing tanks could be carried in addition to the external centerline tank, enabling ferry flights of up to 1,800 miles to be flown. The Gardeniya-1FU active ECM system was not installed, nor was the N-019M radar. Instead a slightly downgraded version of the N-019M, the N-019ME, was fitted. Precisely what was changed is not exactly clear, but the R-77 AAM can be used with this radar. The ability to engage two targets simultaneously was also retained. The cockpit and instrument markings are in English with appropriate units of measurement, and the navigation system, elements of the radio equipment, and other avionics are from western manufacturers. Why no active ECM system and a downgraded version of the N-019M were installed is not clear. Perhaps the customer did not need this or that system, resulting in a lower price for a MiG-29SD. Other notions, such as espionage by a third state would be pure speculation. In any case the MiG-29SD was sold to Malaysia.

MiG-29SE 9.13SE

This variant carries the same radar and weapons system as the MiG-29SD but has an active ECM system, the Gardeniya-1FUE (which is probably slightly downgraded). The weapons load is similar to that of the MiG-29S. Another difference is the presence of the larger bulged fuselage spine, taken from the MiG-29 9.13 Fatback.

Prototype of the retrofit refueling probe, part of the SD program for Malaysia, here connected to the refueling hose of an Il-78 tanker. *RAC MiG*

Close-up of the refueling probe. In front of the probe is the old badge of the guards units of the USSR.

MiG-29SM 9.12SM

Conflicting information in the aeronautical press makes it difficult to say whether the MiG-29SM is based on the 9.12 or 9.13 variant, but it seems most likely that the SM configuration is possible for both versions. What is known for certain is that further improvements in the weapons system make it possible for the aircraft to use TV-guided weapons like the Ch-29T missile and KAB-500Kr guided bomb. The N-019M was modified to become the N-019ME. The air-to-air mode was further improved and the radar is capable of tracking ten targets, locking onto four, and simultaneously attacking two. In ground mode the radar has ground mapping capability. Over time the avionics were also updated, with the addition of a color display, a GLONASS/GPS system and an ECM pod. The SM is also capable of carrying a laser designating pod for use with laser-guided weapons. The IRST (Infra-red search and track) was likewise improved.

MiG-29M 9.15/M1/M2

Soon after the MiG-29 entered service, the MiG OKB began working on a considerably improved version. These improvements largely affected the weapons system, fuel capacity, flight controls, and reduction of pilot workload. Aerodynamically only small changes were necessary. In particular, the designers wanted to make the MiG-29M capable of employing guided air to ground weapons for the precise engagement of ground targets. Externally at least, the aircraft was almost identical to its predecessors. Otherwise a completely new aircraft, similar to the American F/A-18E/F Super Hornet, was developed. The first prototype, with the Bort number 151, flew in 1986 with OKB MiG's chief test pilot, Valery Menitzki, at the controls. Five more followed, with the last having all of the new systems. This aircraft, Bort number 156, was displayed at numerous air shows after the breakup of the Soviet Union, with the intention of selling this modern aircraft. The following measures were taken to address the original MiG-29's major shortcoming, its inadequate fuel capacity: the intake louvers on top of the leading edge root extensions were deleted and replaced by lowering mesh screens in the air intakes (like those of the Su-27). As well, perforated grids were installed in each main undercarriage bay to compensate for the somewhat reduced air flow when the mesh screens were lowered. The screen appears to be very thick in the photo,

Folding grate in the air intake of a MiG-29 with the fine, difficult to make out wire screen.

but this is deceptive, as the fine-meshed screen can barely be seen.

Deletion of the intake louvers with their operating mechanisms created space for 343 gallons of fuel. Further weight was saved through the use of aluminum-lithium alloy, especially in the forward fuselage, and by welding components instead of riveting. As a result of these weight savings, range on internal fuel was increased by approximately 620 miles. A refueling probe was not fitted, as range was considered adequate after the redesign. The heart of the new weapons system was the Zhuk pulse-Doppler radar, which could simultaneously engage four of ten tracked targets. While the N-019 of the older MiG-29 could also track ten targets, it could only engage one. Vertical beam steering is accomplished electronically, while horizontal steering is carried out mechanically. In addition to the air mode, the radar also operates in ground mode and can produce synthetic radar maps of the ground and can be used as a ground tracking radar. Search range is improved by about 30%, weight dropped by about 225 pounds to 485 pounds. The LR/IRST was also modified and is capable of detecting heat sources up to 21.75 miles. A TV sensor is now also available which can identify targets at up to ten kilometers.

The increased use of composite materials, especially in the vertical tail surfaces, the air intakes and the engine fairings, and the application of a radar-absorbing external finish, the radar reflecting area of the original MiG-29 (Fulcrum A) was reduced from 161 square feet to just 16! Aerodynamically, not many changes were needed, as the

Sixth and last prototype (Bort number 156) of the 9.15 variant, seen here at the Farnborough air show in 1992. The Bort numbers worn by the prototypes consisted of the internal designation used by MiG (here product 9.15) with the addition of the prototype number (6 = the 6th prototype). This resulted in the Bort number 156; the 9 was dropped as this generally stood for the MiG-29. *Bernie Condon*

older MiG-29's performance was quite outstanding. The most apparent changes were the sharp edges of the leading edge root extensions, which at high angles of attack produce energy-rich vortices, making the aircraft more controllable and ensuring sufficient lift.

In addition, the trailing edges of the vertical tails beneath the rudders were extended so that both trailing edges are in line. The all-moving tailplanes were also made larger with a sawtooth leading edge to improve controllability. To further improve maneuverability, a Fly-by-Wire system was integrated, although it is purely analogue. The channel for control about the lateral axis (?) is designed as an analogue system with no redundant mechanical systems. Control about the longitudinal and vertical axes is also analogue, but with redundant mechanical systems. These control rods are meant to serve as a mechanical backup

system in case of electrical failure. As is known, the advantage of a fly-by-wire system is that it provides precise control with less force expenditure and smaller movements of the control stick, and the absence of control rods results in a weight saving. The MiG-29M, however, still has control rods, which leads to the conclusion that the designers apparently had no desire to run any risks where the fly-by-wire system was concerned.

Other changes include the speed brake and the braking parachute. The single braking parachute (183 square feet) was replaced by two smaller chutes (each 140 square feet), at least this could be read in publications. In photos of the MiG-29OVT or the MiG-35, however, just one braking parachute can be seen in aircraft photographed while landing, albeit in a slightly modified form. The formerly two-part speed brake, which opened upward and downward, was replaced by a single upward-opening version that is located somewhat further forward. Furthermore the dorsal hump has become larger, extending from the cockpit to the tail, as additional avionics are housed there. The navigation system was improved and a long-range system is now integrated with it. The antenna for the improved radio compass is integrated with the cockpit canopy.

The flare-chaff dispensers and the boundary layer fences forward of the vertical stabilizer roots were also no longer to be found. The flare and chaff dispensers were now in the "beaver tail" between the engines and the number of decoys was doubled to 120. In the wing tips were the antennas of an improved version of the Gardeniya-1FU ECM system. The Gardeniya-1FU acted as an active ECM transmitter and passively in cooperation with the decoys. To compensate for the somewhat greater weight caused by the increased fuel capacity, extensive avionics, and increased weapons load (while retaining the maneuverability of the old MiG-29), it was unavoidable that the engines had to produce more thrust. The result was the RD-33K, which produced 19,333 pounds of thrust, while fuel consumption in full afterburner was approximately seven percent less. Control of the engines was now purely digital by means of an FADEC system (Full Authority Digital Engine Control) that was designed with built-in redundancy. Such a system ensures better efficiency and the engines react more quickly to control inputs by the pilot, as the electronics work faster than hydromechanics. To ensure an adequate supply of air to the engines at high angles of attack, the bottom edges of the intakes were made movable so as to better direct the flow of air into the intakes. The MiG-29M's combat capability

was further increased by increasing the number of weapons stations from six to eight and increasing weapons load from an initial 5,070 pounds to 9,920 pounds. Reinforcement of the wing and the new weapons system made it possible for the MiG-29M to use the most modern guided Russian (and Soviet) air-to-air and air-to-ground missiles, such as the R-77 and all variants of the Ch-25, Ch-29, Ch-31, Ch-35, and TV-guided bombs (with the exception of 3,300-pound bombs). If it was necessary to attack ground targets at night or in bad weather, an appropriate pod with the necessary optical systems could be carried. Of course all normal weapons could be used.

The ammunition supply for the cannon was reduced from 150 to 100 rounds. This was seen as fully adequate for emergency situations, as experience had shown that four to six projectiles were sufficient to take out an enemy fighter aircraft. The changed radar warning equipment made it possible for the now usable Ch-31P to transmit target coordinates of an enemy radar source, if the MiG-29 is to be illuminated by such a radar. Thus the radar could be attacked immediately. To reduce pilot workload, two single-color multifunction displays (cathode ray tubes) were integrated into the cockpit, considerably reducing the number of round analogue instruments. Nevertheless, the

Bort number 155 portrays the fifth prototype, here with operational weapons (from l. to r.) Kh-31, Kh-29T, and R-77. The extended trailing edge of the vertical tail is also evident. Note the more oval shape of the radome, caused by the Zhuk N-010 radar beneath it. The sharp leading edge of the wing can also be seen. *Trevor Hall*

most relevant flight instruments were retained in analogue form for redundancy. The HOTAS (Hands on Throttle and Stick) concept was also perfected, enabling significantly more functions to be controlled from the control stick or throttle lever, without the pilot having to take his hand off one or the other. The ejection seat was placed in a more reclined position to take further loads off the pilot. It was also positioned somewhat higher for a better all-round view. The cockpit canopy was somewhat more bulged than on previous versions.

The prototype of the 9.15 series was subsequently used in development of the MiG-29M2, MiG-29OVT, and the MiG-35. With the development of the new MiG-29K (9.41/47) and MiG-35, MiG decided to also offer a variant which represented a land-based version of the MiG-29K. Designated MiG-29M1 (single-seater, 7.41) and MiG-29M2 (two-seater, 7.47), this variant was largely similar to the naval variant. This was intended to standardize future production, in order to reduce costs. It is outwardly recognizable by its greater wing area (especially the landing flaps), the air intake at the rear of the fuselage bulge in the area of the vertical stabilizers and its radome, which is larger than that of the MiG-35. Missing are the arrestor hook and wing-folding mechanism, even though the bulges associated with the wing fold mechanism are still present on the upper surfaces and undersides of the prototype's wing. Equipment state is largely comparable to the K version, and naval-type components have not been removed. The electronic equipment is also almost identical, although only Russian equipment is used. The chaff/flare dispensers are now located on the aft sections of the engine fairings.

MiG-29K 9.31/9.41/9.47

Development of the MiG-29K was the result of a military requirement for a replacement for the Yak-38 VTOL aircraft, which operated from *Kiev* Class aircraft-carrying cruisers. The combat capabilities of the Yak-38 were so limited that it could never have been a serious opponent. When the search for a replacement began, consideration was initially given to modified versions of the MiG-23 and Su-17, however it was soon decided to select the newest generation of Soviet fighter aircraft. It was also clear that the *Kiev* Class vessels could not simply be modified and that a new design was required. Project 1143.5 (designation for the new aircraft carrier) dispensed with steam catapults (this would probably have delayed production further, for they were already behind schedule) and instead

the carrier was fitted with a ski jump on the bow (similar to the former British *Invincible* Class aircraft carriers) with which to get the aircraft airborne in the available distance. A ski jump and arrestor gear were recreated in the Crimea for carrier flight training. The seventh prototype with the number 918 was used for these trials and all non-vital equipment was removed from the MiG-29 to save weight. The aircraft was also fitted with an arrestor hook, however the undercarriage was not strengthened. Given the designation MiG-29KWP, this aircraft took off from the ski jump for the first time in 1982, with Aviard Fastovets at the controls. This machine enabled valuable lessons to be learned for future pilots. Incidentally the Su-27K and the Su-25UTG also used this training and testing complex.

The operational spectrum of the MiG-29K was not limited to gaining air superiority like the Su-27K or Su-33, but also included attacks against enemy vessels, which made it a multirole aircraft. From a technological standpoint the MiG-29K was a naval version of the MiG-29M, however some modifications were carried out to adapt it to conditions at sea. First of all the undercarriage was beefed up to withstand carrier landings. Tire pressure was also increased. The nosewheel leg's pivot angle was also increased to ninety degrees to either side to improve its ability to maneuver on the deck of the carrier. There is also a lamp on the nosewheel leg which serves to visually transmit important information about the position and speed of the aircraft to the deck landing officer while on approach.

Special attention was paid to anticorrosion protection, as sensitive aircraft components did not stand up well to the raw ocean climate. An arrestor hook was also added as were folding mechanisms for the wings and radome (the latter is no longer mentioned in newer publications and may have been abandoned). These features reduce wingspan to 25.5 feet and overall length to 49.5 feet (possibly, see above). As a braking parachute cannot be used, the chaff/flare dispenser is positioned in the "beaver tail" of the dorsal spine, and an over-fuselage air brake roughly between the vertical stabilizers, which was taken from the 9.15.

In contrast to the MiG-29M, it was necessary to increase the K-version's wing area by about 54 square feet, for with the sharply-reduced takeoff distance from the carrier, operations with the original wing area would have been associated with unacceptable performance losses and risks. The engines were also changed, to satisfy the demands of a shortened takeoff run. Basically they were the same RD-33Ks as those of the MiG-29M, with the difference that when taking off from a carrier deck a higher thrust setting could be selected from the fully digital engine control system to guarantee a safe takeoff. There are two different takeoff

MiG-29K 9.41
with 300-gallon
fuel tanks
beneath the
wings. *Press
Office UAC*

Second
prototype 312 of
the 9.31 version
with folded
wings and R-73
simulators. The
white flag on the
tail identifies the
aircraft as
belonging to the
Russian Navy.
Unlike 311,
aircraft 312 had
a dark grey
finish on its
upper surfaces.

positions on the deck, two forward for normally loaded aircraft and another for fully loaded machines. The forward positions have a takeoff distance of 345 feet and the rear one offers 640 feet. Even though the internal fuel capacity of the MiG-29M was greatly increased, it was nevertheless decided to equip the MiG-29K with a retractable refueling probe. With the UPAZ-K refueling pod, the MiG-29K can also deliver fuel to other combat aircraft, eliminating the need for specialized tankers.

The weapons and navigation systems were optimized for operations over water and differ from those of the MiG-29M only in these respects. Additional radio and navigation equipment was integrated and serves as an interface between the MiG-29K and the carrier. The control system has also remained unchanged. An interesting change was undertaken with respect to the ejection seat: if the pilot ejects from the aircraft while on the deck of the carrier, he is fired 30 degrees to the side and thus lands safely in the water and not on the deck. This also gives the parachute a few more meters to deploy.

The MiG-29K flew for the first time in June 1988, with test pilot Toktar Aubarikov at the controls. After several test flights it was flown to the NITKA complex in the Crimea, where it underwent extensive trials. This complex reproduces

the deck of the aircraft carrier *Tbilisi* on the ground. Numerous takeoffs and landings had to be carried out on this ground complex before deck trials began. Tests included arrested carrier landings, wave-offs with increased engine power, landing approach with the approach system, and similar procedures. The launch point looked as follows: retractable restraining wedges for the main undercarriage wheels, to fix the aircraft while the engines achieved full power. To divert jet blast upwards, a water-cooled thrust deflector in the form of a large plate was set up behind the aircraft. On November 1, 1989, the MiG-29K landed on the carrier *Tbilisi*, the second aircraft to do so after the Su-27K. It was, however, the first aircraft to take off from this carrier.

The second prototype was used largely to test the avionics. During deck trials cracks were discovered on the first prototype's undercarriage and the aircraft had to undergo repairs. After a total of 320 flights with seventy-four carrier landings, the test program was halted before it could be completed. The reason was the collapse of the Soviet Union and all that that entailed. This is seen as the reason why only the Su-27K was introduced as a carrier aircraft, for its test program was completed, having begun earlier. Nevertheless, this decision is not particularly illuminating, for the MiG-29K is capable of air and ground

312 with extended refueling probe. The markings beneath the windscreen indicate the number of successful deck landings and takeoffs.

Aircraft 311 landing on the Soviet carrier *Tbilisi. Alexey Micheyev*

attacks with modern and effective guided weapons, while the Su-27K lacks any significant ground attack (or naval strike) capability (sole exception: when carrying the Ch-41 MOSKIT, only one of which can be carried because of its size). Because of its larger size, fewer Su-27Ks can be taken on board. Whether the Su-27K's other advantages, such as greater range, higher thrust-to-weight ratio, and two additional hardpoints, offset the MiG-29K's advantages remains to be seen, for operational experience with the Su-27K has not been entirely satisfactory.

The Russian Navy has begun correcting this situation and the latest MiG-29K variants are being procured for the *Admiral Kuznetsov*. In 2004, India procured the aircraft-carrying cruiser *Admiral Gorschkov* (*Kiev* Class), formerly the *Baku*, for 700 million US dollars, and with Russian help it was converted into a pure aircraft carrier. The *Baku* was the fourth *Kiev* Class carrier, but with considerable improvements. The most obvious feature was the completely new island, with a phased antenna on each side. This island was adopted virtually unchanged for the *Admiral Kuznetsov*.

The *Baku* was originally built as a carrier for the new Yak-41. The Yak-41 was the world's second supersonic VTOL aircraft. There was a serious incident during trials, in which the prototype was badly damaged. Despite this, the test program aboard the *Baku* was completed successfully. After the collapse of the Soviet Union, however, there was no funding with which to produce the Yak-41 in quantity for service with the fleet. The *Baku* became a helicopter carrier and was sold to India in 2004. The conversion work undertaken on the *Baku* by the Indians was intended to result in a carrier similar to the *Admiral Kuznetsov*.

Twelve MiG-29Ks (9.41) and four MiG-29KUBs (9.47) were initially procured for service from the carrier, and twenty-nine additional aircraft were later delivered to India. Now called the MiG-33, these aircraft were developed versions of the MiG-29K (9.31) with avionics similar to those of the MiG-29M1/M2. Special attention was paid to the electronics, with the Zhuk-ME, which had been used by the MiG-29SMT 9.19, forming the heart of the system.

The BK-DU-130 onboard oxygen generating system made by the Zvezda Company was used in a Russian combat aircraft for the first time and it was first tested in the MiG-29M2 in 2005. Emergency oxygen bottles were installed, but the oxygen generator provided a permanent supply. A French GPS navigation system and a helmet sight, Israeli ECM systems. and Indian communications equipment completed the avionics. As there are single- and two-seat variants, the pilots have three and the weapons system officer (WSO) four Russian-made color displays. It is noteworthy that both versions have the same canopy,

with an additional fuel tank installed in the rear cockpit of the single-seat version. The installed power plants are Klimov RD-33MKs, but without thrust vectoring nozzles. A new accessory gearbox is also used, also for the first time. While all previous MiG-29s had a central accessory gearbox, now two gearboxes are combined in one, the KSA-33M. Almost all of the generator units of the old KSA-2/3 (fuel and hydraulic pumps, direct and alternating current generators, engine power units) were doubled. The KSA-33M is still centrally mounted and is powered by both engines. Here, too, a single engine can power the two internal gearboxes. This new gearbox considerably improves failure safety, although it weighs 183 pounds more. On the lengthened wing roots there are now small flaps that are only extended on landing and serve as high-lift devices. Also new is a retractable boarding ladder in the left wing root extension.

Also new is the K-36D-3.5 ejection seat, which replaces the K-36DM, which was itself extremely efficient. Airframe life is 6,000 hours or forty years. The maiden flight of the MiG-29KUB took place in January 2007, and deliveries of the first sixteen MiGs to the Indian Navy began two years later. The NITKA complex in the Crimea was reactivated and modernized for testing of the new naval version. This was not possible until the reelection of Viktor Yanukovych, who strove for better relations with Russian than his predecessor Viktor Yushchenko. Yanukovych arranged a lease with Russia for use of the former Black Sea port and installations in the Crimea, which had their origins in the days of the Soviet Union.

That same year extensive deck trials took place on board the *Admiral Kuznetsov*. Deck trials on the *Vikramadtya*, which was now completed, began in 2012, with two MiG-29K and KUB aircraft.

Altogether the conversion and modernization of the former aircraft-carrying cruiser *Baku* (*Minsk* Class) took nine years. The price of roughly 750 million US dollars originally negotiated in 2004, ultimately doubled. Russian obligated itself to a one-year guarantee and twenty-year maintenance package for the aircraft carrier. In 2013, the completed *Vikramadtya* was officially handed over to the Indian Navy. A complex similar to the NITKA complex in the Crimea was established in India for ground training of the Indian MiG-29 pilots, and a similar one was built in China for its aircraft carrier. At the beginning of 2012, MiG signed a contract with the Russian government for delivery of twenty MiG-29Ks and four MiG-29KUBs for the aircraft carrier *Admiral Kuznetsov* of the Northern Fleet. In November 2013, the Russian Navy received the first four of a total of twenty-four MiG-29 KUBs.

MiG-29K 9.47 with refueling hose and Paz-MK refueling pack. The hose extends roughly sixty-two feet and is capable of transferring up to 198 gallons of fuel per minute.

In November 2016, the aircraft carrier *Admiral Kuznetsov* was in the Mediterranean to provide support for Syrian government forces in their struggle against ISIS. Aboard the carrier were Su-27K and MiG-29K fighters of the 100th Independent Fighter Aviation Regiment. One MiG-29K crashed but the crew ejected and survived. Prior to this the arrestor gear had been damaged and the MiG still in the air was unable to recover. An attempt was made to repair the damage and the MiG's pilot was refused permission to proceed to a base on the mainland. The inevitable happened: the damage could not be repaired and the MiG ran out of fuel. The aircraft crashed into the sea. A similar crash, this time by a Su-27K, took place one month later. The Russians did not reveal whether the damage had been caused by the arrestor system itself or by a mistake during landings.

Indian KUB and Russian K during deck trials on the *Admiral Kuznetsov*. RAC MiG

9.41 with extended LERX flap (directly above the air intake). On close examination it is possible to make out the zigzag pattern at the edge of the radome, which is suggestive of a stealth measure. *Vladislav Perminov*

115

MiG-29KUB photographed in the early morning. The extended flaps (see arrow) indicate that the aircraft is landing, as they are only deployed for landing. *RAC MiG*

The single-seater during trials with the Kh-35. It is also loaded with external tanks and R-73 AAMs. Here, too, the zigzag pattern on the radome can be seen. *RAC MiG*

The MiG-29K in its original special paint scheme. *RAC MiG – Katsuhiko Tokunaga*

MiG-29K ready for landing. *RAC MiG – Katsuhiko Tokunaga*

Russian
MiG-29KUB
about to land on
the deck of the
*Admiral
Kuznetsov*. The
white circle on
the deck marks
a landing point
for Ka-27
helicopters,
while the
structure in the
background is
the landing flight
coordinator's
control position.
RAC MiG

Just landed on the *Admiral Kuznetsov*. The aircraft has taken the middle arrestor cable. The crew is wearing special sea survival suits, which are required by regulations when operating over water. *RAC MiG*

Full afterburner, but the restraining shoes are still blocking the aircraft. At any moment the shoes will fold forward, releasing the aircraft for takeoff. *Press Office UAC*

Here the restraining shoes are still up. A refueling pack is on the centerline station and the underwing racks have four 300-gallon external tanks. *RAC MiG*

Indian KUB on the stern of the *Admiral Kuznetsov* during deck trials. *RAC MiG*

The single-seater during an afterburner takeoff from the *Vikramaditya*. *RAC MiG*

KUB during
afterburner
takeoff from the
Vikramaditya,
identifiable by
the English
lettering on the
deck. *RAC MiG*

Cockpit of the
9.41,
photographed
in 2005.

MiG-29SMT 9.17/9.18/9.19

When Russian was unable to procure the modern MiG-29M due to lack of funding after the fall of the Soviet Union, the air force saw itself falling behind. Its MiGs still lacked adequate range and the entire electronics suite was obsolete, consequently there was only one choice, to modernize its existing MiG-29s: the MiG-29SMT was born. In the beginning, the intention was to integrate many elements of the MiG-29M, however this was frustrated by high costs. And so only the fuselage spine was made larger, this accommodating approximately 3,300 pounds of fuel, and the speed brake from the MiG-29M was adopted. A refueling probe could be fitted if required. Some changes were made to the aircraft's avionics. The most obvious were two large multifunction displays and a digital input unit on the console. The HOTAS principle was exploited, while key analogue backup instruments were retained. The N-019MP radar was initially installed, which compared to the N-109M was capable of producing ground radar maps with a resolution of fifty feet. The resulting maps could be transmitted to ground stations in real time by satellite. The

optical target search system and the helmet-mounted sight remained part of the aircraft's equipment. The navigation system consists of a laser gyroscope and GPS system. The new avionics resulted in a weight savings of about 1,320 pounds. After a wide variety of systems were tested in several previous prototypes, the first flight of the fully equipped MiG-29SMT took place in 1998. All of the systems described above were installed in this aircraft and it was in fact equivalent to the actual project MiG-29SMT. The SMT was capable of using laser- and television-guided weapons as well as anti-radar guided missiles and the R-77 AAM.

The designers were not finished improving the aircraft's performance, however and the result was the MiG-29SMT2. As was so often the case, the aircraft's radar played a decisive role. The N-019MP was replaced by the Zhuk N-010M and it by the Zhuk-ME. The latter had an increased range of seventy-five miles and could detect and attack helicopters hovering near ground level. The radar was capable of tracking ten targets and attacking four simultaneously. The entire array of modern guided air-to-ground weapons was now also usable. A radar-absorbing outer finish and new materials reduced the aircraft's radar

Prototype of the 9.19 version. The new paint scheme with straight lines is eye-catching and is supposed to break up the shape of the aircraft more effectively. The much modified dorsal hump is obvious. The aircraft is carrying radar-guided R-77 AAMs and Kab-500Kr TV-guided bombs.
RAC MiG – Katsuhiko Tokunaga

The SMT, photographed in 2005.

SMT 9.17
cockpit with
color displays,
photographed
in 2005.

signature by a factor of 15 to just 16 square feet. It would later be possible to use the RD-33MK, envisaged for the MiG-29K/M and the MiG-35, to compensate for the aircraft's higher weight. Initially, the RD-33 Series 3 engines were installed, which had a greater operating life of 2,000 hours. The 9.17 was abandoned in favor of the 9.19. In 2002 a contract was signed with Yemen for the procurement of twelve SMT 9.18 fighters (four new-build aircraft and eight converted 9.12s) and these were delivered in 2005. Eritrea received two MiG-29SMT 9.18 fighters the same year. The MiG-29SMT 9.18 was a series 9.12 airframe without the typical larger dorsal spine with the avionics of the SMT 9.17-II. Another export customer was Algeria, which in 2006 signed a contract for twenty-eight examples of the MiG-29SMT 9.19 and six MiG-29UBT 9.52 two-seaters worth approximately 1.3 billion US dollars. On this version of the SMT the fuselage tank of the 9.17 version was shortened

to reduce the danger of a fuel fire in the event of a compressor blade failure in one of the engines, as the tank was located between the engines.

Fifteen aircraft were delivered between 2006 and May 2007. Then Algeria stopped its payments, as Algerian engineers had discovered issues with manufacturing quality, claiming that used materials and in some cases airframes had been used. RSK MiG responded that the aircraft were new-build and that Algerian technicians had checked out and accepted the aircraft before they entered service. Ultimately, however, Russia took back the fifteen aircraft that had been delivered and the contract was cancelled. The aircraft were then taken on strength by the Russian Air Force. The Russian Air Force ultimately received twenty-eight SMT and six UBT two-seat trainers. In 2014, a contract was signed for a further sixteen SMT to be delivered by 2016.

The SMT 9.18 was delivered to several African states with an appropriate camouflage scheme. This photo was taken during the Dubai Air Show in 2005. *Steve Brimley*

Prototype of the SMT 9.19 with the Bort number 777, carrying KAB-500Kr guided bombs and R-77 AAMs. The dorsal hump typical of this version can be seen here. *RAC MiG – Katsuhiko Tokunaga*

The 9.19 in its unique camouflage scheme. The type was painted in different colors for the Russian Air Force. *RAC MiG – Katsuhiko Tokunaga*

The 9.19
prototype with
the Bort number
777 was a
converted 9.12.
*RAC MiG –
Katsuhiko
Tokunaga*

From this perspective, the aircraft's camouflage finish is causing parts of its external contours to merge with the background. *RAC MiG – Katsuhiko Tokunaga*

SMT 9.19 in service with the Russian Air Force. Beneath the starboard wing is a B-8 rocket pod containing twenty 80 mm (3.15 inch) unguided rockets. *Patrick Bigel*

MiG-35

The MiG-35 is the most modern variant of the MiG-29 and is in the running for an Indian Air Force requirement for up to 126 medium combat aircraft. The prototype MiG-29M2 (not to be confused with the MiG-29M2 9.67) took to the air for the first time on September 26, 2001. This prototype used the airframe of the fourth MiG-29M prototype, as revealed by the number 154 at the top of the fin, however the forward fuselage had to be redesigned because of the second crewmember and the installation of a full-fledged radar.

If the MiG-35 does enter production, the lithium alloy used in the MiG-29M/-K (9.15/9.31) will not be used. The associated costs can no longer be justified, as the resulting weight saving is just 175 pounds. Models of the MiG-35 at displays also exhibit changes to the airframe, such as larger wings and vertical tails as well as eleven stores hardpoints. Whether these changes will make their way to the production version is questionable, for efforts are being made to keep production costs as low as possible by standardizing the different versions (airframes) to the maximum possible degree. The avionics

include the most modern equipment from Russian and foreign sources. The cockpit has been radically modernized and now can be described as an all-glass cockpit. The pilot has three and the weapons operator four multifunction displays of Russian origin. There are dual controls to allow the WSO to fly the aircraft if necessary. As the forward view from the rear cockpit is poor, a video camera image is displayed on the center display. The HOTAS principle is further improved. A satellite-based system is also integrated into the navigation system. The key element of the new variant is undoubtedly the Zhuk-AE radar by Phazotron. It has an active electronically scanned array, with the radar beam controlled electronically instead of by moving the antenna. This enables more targets to be tracked that are farther apart and in much less time. The MiG-35 is identifiable by the Zhuk-AE's smaller radome.

The original antenna was larger (27.5 inches) and complete with processors that weighed more than 880 pounds, which was too much for an aircraft of this size. Range was initially 120 miles, but after the reduction of the number of individual phase modules this fell to 100 miles. The radar can track thirty targets and attack eight simultaneously. In the near future it will most probably

MiG-29 with Zhuk AE radar, identifiable by its smaller radome.

Named the MiG-29M2 in 2001, this aircraft was converted from the fourth prototype of the MiG-29M 9.15, recognizable from the Bort number 154. The letters MRCA on the vertical tail indicate Multi Role Combat Aircraft.

Photographed in 2005, a MiG-29M2 with smoke
generators under its wings, which were designed
for use at air displays. The larger radome of the
Zhuk ME radar can be seen in this photo.

Now renamed MiG-35, this aircraft has the complete optronics package. Most conspicuous is the lower IRST on the starboard engine fairing. The smaller radome houses the Zhuk AE radar. The MiG is carrying a representative weapons load of R-73 and R-77 AAMs plus Kab-500Kr guided bombs. *RAC MiG – Katsuhiko Tokunaga*

The prototype MiG-35 was also developed from a prototype of the MiG-29 9.15. The Bort number 154 shows that the aircraft was the fourth prototype of the 9.15. *RAC MiG – Katsuhiko Tokunaga*

The cockpit configuration differs from that of the Su-30 in that the rear seat fore the weapons officer is not as raised in the MiG as in the two-seat Sukhois and thus minimizes the height of the canopy. *RAC MiG – Katsuhiko Tokunaga*

The separation
between the
wing and the
engine pods is
particularly
noticeable here.
*RAC MiG –
Katsuhiko
Tokunaga*

MiG-35 with full weapons load. Unlike the Su-27, the MiG is unable to carry weapons between the air intakes. *RAC MiG – Katsuhiko Tokunaga*

The MiG-35
inherited its
larger
saw-tooth
tailerons
from the
9.15. *RAC
MiG
– Katsuhiko
Tokunaga*

be possible to drastically increase the number of antenna modules, resulting in an increase in range and number of targets that can be tracked. Defense systems include active ECM equipment from Israel and a passive optical system from Russia. The detection range of the IRST/ LR was improved (to twenty-eight miles) and a helmet-mounted sight from either France or Russia can be used. There is also an IRST/LR under the starboard engine fairing for ground targets, which can be detected and tracked at ranges up to twenty-five miles. Beneath the port engine fairing is a missile warning device, and another is located just behind the canopy. Incoming air-to-air missiles are detected at ranges of up to eighteen miles, air-to-ground missiles at up to thirty miles and shoulder-launched surface-to-air missiles at up to ten miles. Laser detectors are installed in both wing tips, warning the pilot of range finders in enemy fighters at ranges up to eighteen miles. All of these systems provide the MiG-35 with excellent all-round defense capability. Should a missile nevertheless get through, there is a chaff-flare dispenser. A new feature is a towed radar decoy system. The decoy is deployed on a cable up to 450 feet behind the aircraft and fools the incoming missile into believing it to be a real aircraft (weight 12 pounds).

The White Russian company 558 Aircraft Repair Plant JSC offers one more alternative. Called Satellite, it is an active ECM system that transmits false targets to enemy radars in the form of radar echoes from the carrier aircraft. This causes several targets to appear on the enemy radar, making it impossible to say which one is real. The device resembles an external store and is mounted on a stores rack, which remains capable of carrying a weapon.

The communications system comes from India. The following is extremely interesting with respect to defense measures: in 1999, it was announced that the Russian Keldysh Research Institute had developed a plasma generator, which generated a plasma field around an aircraft. This plasma field absorbs radar waves, making it impossible to locate the aircraft. This device is believed to have been tested on a Su-27 in 2002, and the reflected radar waves were completely neutralized. Whether or not the carrier aircraft can use its own radar is not known. The generator weighs about 220 pounds and is supposedly already available for the MiG-35 and Su-35.

As the MiG-35's gross weight is clearly higher (all told the MiG-35 weighs about two tons more than the MiG-29M/-K 9.15/31), new, more powerful engines were required to maintain the aircraft's well-known

IRST sensor on the underside of the starboard engine fairing.

Far right: towed radar decoy used by the MiG-35.

The Zhuk AE fixed antenna radar. Compared to the NO-19, the radar's compactness is striking.

Here the MiG-35 is shown in a simulated refueling from a MiG-29K 9.41 (with four 300-gallon underwing tanks). *Weimeng*

maneuverability. And so the RD-33MK was installed, with its improved performance, economy ,and operating life (see the chapter on the MiG-29OVT). The increased weight is largely due to the aircraft's increased fuel capacity (10,360 lb.), weapons load (14,300 lb.), and the added cockpit for the second crewmember. The MiG-35 also has a refueling probe similar to that of the MiG-29K.

All Russian weapons suitable for an aircraft of this size can be carried, such as the Ch-29, Ch-31, Ch-35, laser- and television-guided bombs, R-27, R-77, R-73, and a large variety of unguided weapons. If the customer desires, western weapons can also be integrated into the weapons system. Another important innovation concerns the Fly-by-Wire control system that is now fully digital and not partly analogue (or partly digital) as on the MiG-29M/K. The pilot can set the sensitivity of the control elements individually. Airframe time is at least forty years or about 6,000 flying hours.

The MiG-35's chances of becoming the new fighter for the Indian Air Force ended in 2011, when the Dassault Rafale was named the winner. Concrete reasons why MiG lost out were not officially given, but it was suspected that is in part due to the transfer of the latest non-Russian technology, for the contract included provisions for the licensed production of at least some components, which made the transfer of technology possible. The MiG-35 is under discussion for procurement by the Russian Air Force, however this has been delayed repeatedly. Whether the Russian Air Force will place its future entirely on the T-50 or is working in secret on a successor to the MiG-29 remains to be seen.

At the beginning of 2017, RAC MiG demonstrated a new MiG-35. It was based on the airframe of the MiG-29K/KUB. The wing of the carrier version was adopted, though without the wing fold mechanism. The avionics were improved, the displays having better resolution and faster operating speed. The self-defense system was expanded, including additional radar warning sensors forward of the cockpit glazing, on the side of the fuselage nose, behind the canopy and underneath the fuselage nose, providing better all-round coverage. Unlike the Su-35S, for example, the missile warning system consists of infrared modules instead of UV ones. In the cockpit the crew is shown the position of incoming missiles. The laser warning sensors in the wing tips were retained. The most important innovation seems to be the aircraft's radar. The Zhuk-AE prototype radar has been further developed to produce the Zhuk-AME. Range and number of targets are about the same, but the size of the radar appears to have been reduced. The aircraft is offered

with a Russian-made targeting pod. It contains a thermal imaging system and a laser tracker/illuminator/range finder/warning system plus a television camera. The pod can track four ground targets simultaneously. The pod is mounted beneath one of the air intakes and replaces the one previously carried by the MiG-35 (OLS-K). This modernized MiG-35 is again being offered to India, as it only negotiated the purchase of forty Rafales from France. It is expected that after positive trials with the MiG-35, which are to last until the summer of 2017, the Russian Air Force will replace its entire MiG-29 fleet with the MiG-35.

MiG-29UB 9.51 – UB 9.52

Ever since the MiG-9, in addition to the pure combat version of its fighter aircraft, the OKB MiG has always developed a two-seat training version in parallel. The MiG-29 was no exception. It was believed that a two-seat version was the best possible way of converting or training pilots. Aviard Fastovets took the MiG-29UB into the air on its maiden flight in 1981, and three prototypes completed the test program without incident. To minimize the number of required design changes no radar was fitted, although the aircraft had a radar range finder. The space freed up as a result was used for the trainee pilot's cockpit. The flight instructor sat in the rear cockpit.

As forward visibility from the rear seat was restricted by the trainee pilot's seat, a retractable periscope was installed. The instructor can extend/retract the periscope by pushing a button. There is also a curtain in the trainee pilot's cockpit for instrument flight training.

Fuel capacity is identical to that of the single-seat version, however gross weight is 880 pounds higher. This additional weight has little effect on performance. Strictly speaking, the two-seat MiG-29 cannot be called a combat aircraft, for without radar it cannot operate independently and visual procedures had to be used with the IR sensor. Only infrared AAMs can be used, however the long-range version of the R-27 can also only be used in conjunction with other aircraft. Ammunition capacity for the cannon was reduced to fifty rounds. The chaff/flare dispensers at the base of the vertical tails was also deleted. The UB prototypes at first had the ventral fins of the single-seat MiG-29, however these were later deleted after the rudders were enlarged. The same is true of the dirt deflector on the nosewheel, which was later fitted with an FOD screen.

Russian Air
Force MiG-29UB
during final
checks just
before takeoff.
Note the raised
periscope for
the rear cockpit.
*Sergey
Chaikovsky*

Polish MiG-29UB
from Malbork in a
climbing turn in
full afterburner.
Adam Svechovski

Raised periscope atop the canopy for the second crewmember. Also note the fake canopy painted under the fuselage nose. *Stefan Gawlista*

Looking at the lower periscope mirror in the rear cockpit gives the impression that one in fact has a clear view forward. *Stefan Gawlista*

The MiG-29UB is thus a pure training aircraft with only minimal combat capability, and it cannot be considered a true operational aircraft (unlike the UBT). It performs well as a trainer, however, and the instructor is able to simulate a variety of scenarios. Should the student lose control of the aircraft, there is a second set of controls with which the instructor can take control. The MiG-29UB was built in the SOKOL Factory in Nizhni Novgorod.

Thoughts soon turned to modernization of the MiG-29UB as well, in the style of the MiG-29SMT. In the mid-1990s, however, the Russian Air Force was strapped for cash. And so, instead of buying new aircraft, the existing MiG-29UBs were reequipped to become fully combat-capable aircraft. Technically, the UBT was a tremendous step forward compared to the UB. Integration of the OSA-2 fixed-antenna radar meant that the aircraft could carry all available modern air-to-ground and air-to-air weapons. As the size of the MiG-29UBT was to remain the same as the UB, the new radar had to fit in the old aircraft. The company Tikhonurov NIIP handled this requirement very well, for the OSA-2 weighs all of 330 pounds, and its performance can be said to be comparable to that of the N-010 in the old MiG-29M/K and that at half the weight of the earlier radar. The MiG-

MiG-29UB of *JG 73 "Steinhoff"* in the sound protection hangar. The red covers on top of the wing roots are screens, which prevent personnel or other foreign objects from being sucked in.

The rear cockpit of the flight instructor. Above the instrument panel are controls for simulating various situations for the student.

29UBT can thus detect an aerial target at a distance of fifty-three miles, track eight targets, and engage four of them simultaneously. It is also capable of employing laser- and TV-guided precision munitions and medium to long-range air-to-air missiles. In ground mode the OSA-2 is also capable of producing radar maps that are important for the use of weapons or can be used to evaluate the area. Some of the Russian UB machines have been brought to the avionics standard of the SMT, but without radar and a refueling probe.

The number of wing hardpoints has been left at six. However the weapons load has been raised to 9,920 pounds. The UBT made its maiden flight in August 1998. The UBTs delivered to Algeria and later returned were also incorporated into the Russian Air Force. These variants allowed more money to be earned, as they would certainly be more expensive than the UB. This would be regrettable, but the UBT would be a real alternative for countries that have the MiG-29 in service but cannot afford an SMT or more modern type.

Photographed in
1999, a UBT on
display with a
range of
weaponry. Like
the SMT, its
dorsal hump is
quite obvious.

MiG-29OVT

The MiG-29OVT must be seen as a pure technological testbed, as it is not a series prototype but rather is used to test various systems. The idea of equipping the MiG-29 with thrust vectoring goes back to the early 1990s. The aircraft then designated the MiG-33 had canards in addition to thrust vectoring. The thrust vector nozzles were first tested on a test stand in 1997, then in 2003, they were tested in the air by the MiG-29OVT. Apparently, spurred by the sales success of the Su-30MKI, Mikoyan presented the prototype of the MiG-29OVT (albeit a display model) at the MAKS 2001 air show in Moscow. Like the MiG-29M2, it was a converted prototype of the MiG-29M 9.15 (No.156, see pointed vertical tail tips). The aircraft was originally built in 1991, and by the time the project was abandoned in 1993, it had completed about eighty-six test flights and was then stored. With the start of the OVT program in 2001, it was reactivated. Close examination of the nozzles reveals that standard engines were installed and that the then RD-33-10M was not ready for flight trials in 2001. This demonstrated, however, that no particular airframe design changes were required to install the RD-33-10M.

The vector nozzles have a pivot range of 15 degrees in all directions and movement speed is 60 degrees per second. Also new are the launch rails for air-to-air missiles on the wing tips, increasing the number of hardpoints to ten (not counting the under-fuselage rack). These launch rails were then removed during flight trials. At the MAKS 2004 aviation show the OVT was first publicly demonstrated in flight and made a tremendous impression. At ILA 2006, it was said that the engines were RD-33 Series IIs (but with thrust vector nozzles), which at 18,210 pounds of thrust were the less powerful version of the RD-33. The new RD-33MK has been in service since 2005, however. This engine produces approximately 20,200 pounds of thrust, has a smokeless combustion chamber, an emergency fuel jettison system, and improved digital engine controls. The thrust vector nozzles are taken from the RD-33 Series 2, as these are interchangeable. Operating life was increased to 4,000 hours with overhauls scheduled every 1,000 hours. The digital flight controls were adapted to thrust vector control and expanded. The BARS-29 electronically-scanned radar for the OVR was also displayed at MAKS 2005, the first time a MiG-29 was equipped with a radar by Tikhomirov (which previously made radars for the Su-27 family) and not one made by Phazotron.

For its public unveiling the OVT was given a special paint scheme. The vortices over the leading edge root extensions and the active smoke generators can be plainly seen. *Weimeng*

The BARS-29 weighs 550 pounds and is thus about a third lighter than the old NO-19. This radar is capable of tracking fifteen aerial targets and simultaneously engaging four. At ILA 2006, however, there was talk that the Zhuk-ME was to be fitted, but here too there is yet no clear statements. The IRST was removed for the flight tests, and the sensor dome is absent from the front of the cockpit. The MiG-29OVT should be seen as a technology demonstrator for other versions of the MiG-29, created to test different types of equipment.

Capable of pivoting in all directions, the nozzle of the RD-33-10M, as it was then designated (2001).

Installed in the OVT with modified nozzle.

Fixed antenna of the BARS-29 radar.

The OVT carrying smoke generators. *RAC MiG*

This digital camouflage scheme, which is particularly effective over built-up areas, here on a MiG-29 of the Slovakian Air Force. *Petr Pirony*

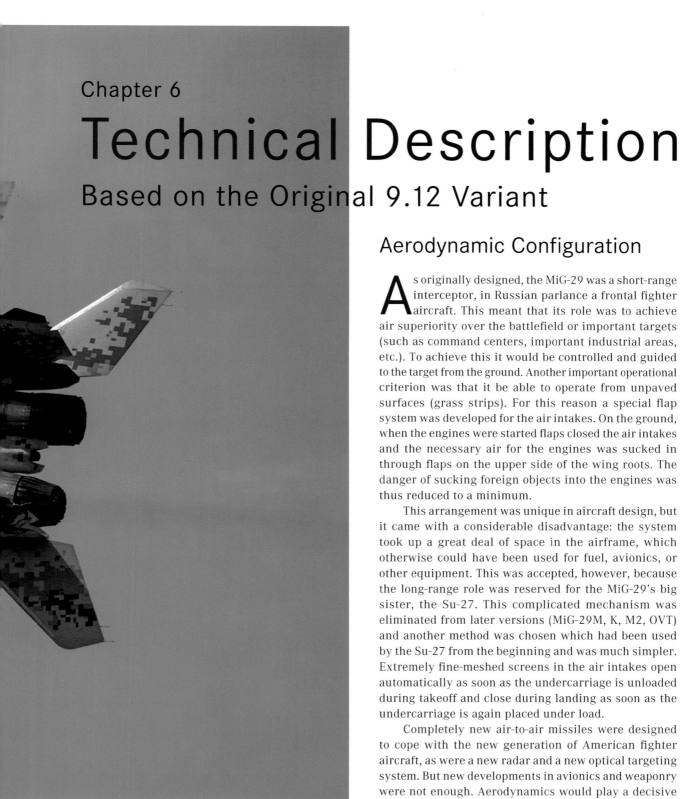

Chapter 6
Technical Description
Based on the Original 9.12 Variant

Aerodynamic Configuration

As originally designed, the MiG-29 was a short-range interceptor, in Russian parlance a frontal fighter aircraft. This meant that its role was to achieve air superiority over the battlefield or important targets (such as command centers, important industrial areas, etc.). To achieve this it would be controlled and guided to the target from the ground. Another important operational criterion was that it be able to operate from unpaved surfaces (grass strips). For this reason a special flap system was developed for the air intakes. On the ground, when the engines were started flaps closed the air intakes and the necessary air for the engines was sucked in through flaps on the upper side of the wing roots. The danger of sucking foreign objects into the engines was thus reduced to a minimum.

This arrangement was unique in aircraft design, but it came with a considerable disadvantage: the system took up a great deal of space in the airframe, which otherwise could have been used for fuel, avionics, or other equipment. This was accepted, however, because the long-range role was reserved for the MiG-29's big sister, the Su-27. This complicated mechanism was eliminated from later versions (MiG-29M, K, M2, OVT) and another method was chosen which had been used by the Su-27 from the beginning and was much simpler. Extremely fine-meshed screens in the air intakes open automatically as soon as the undercarriage is unloaded during takeoff and close during landing as soon as the undercarriage is again placed under load.

Completely new air-to-air missiles were designed to cope with the new generation of American fighter aircraft, as were a new radar and a new optical targeting system. But new developments in avionics and weaponry were not enough. Aerodynamics would play a decisive

The closed main air intakes can be seen in this view. They open automatically at about 120 miles per hour on takeoff. *Stefan Gawlista*

On the ground the engines receive the required air by way of the open intake louvers, called OLEK. This minimizes the danger of ingesting foreign objects. *Stefan Gawlista*

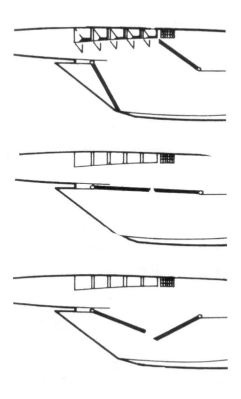

role in the design of the MiG-29. The fuselage, with broad wing roots, was therefore designed as an integrated lifting body, a so-called integral concept. In this design the fuselage produced 40 percent of the lift, which in turn reduced wing loading during turning engagements and ultimately permitted higher g-loads. The leading edge of the wing roots were extended forward to produce energy-rich vortices, which at high angles of attack also produced lift.

The developers chose twin vertical tails, which in contrast to a conventional tail improved longitudinal stability at high angles of attack and reduced overall height. The vertical tail surfaces are canted outwards six degrees. The engines are in separate nacelles with large air intakes beneath the fuselage, ensuring sufficient airflow to the engines even at high angles of attack and tight turns. The selected power plants were to be powerful, while keeping size and weight within acceptable limits. This was necessary for the MiG-29 to achieve the required agility. For the engines had to be powerful enough for their combined maximum thrust to be at least equal to the fighter's normal weight. The RD-33 engine enabled this requirement to be met and its combination with the MiG-29's aerodynamics produced such outstanding

Schematic representation of the different positions of the air intake surfaces. *Matthias Grunder*

The extended roots of the vertical tail surfaces serve as boundary layer fences and as carriers of chaff and flares. The very clear digital camouflage scheme (a variant) of the Slovakian Air Force can be seen very well in this view. *RAC MiG*

results that many practice opponents during NATO and other exercises were extremely surprised by the MiG's capabilities.

An aircraft with two engines also has better survivability. If one engine is put out of action in combat or by a technical fault, the aircraft can be flown back to base or at least to safety. The entire aerodynamics of the MiG are optimized for the subsonic and transonic speed ranges, as most aerial combat takes place in these speed ranges.

Hydraulic System

The hydraulic system consists of a main hydraulic system and a hydraulic boost system. These two systems are installed in separate locations and are thus independent of one another. The following components are hydraulically actuated:

Main and nosewheel undercarriage (lowering and retraction, plus nosewheel steering and braking system when foot-operated)
• Control of the aerodynamic control surfaces
• Speed brakes
• Auxiliary power unit (GTDA-117A) exhaust door
• Control of the upper air intake flaps and the engine air intake ramps

The main system is further broken down into first- and second-level systems. If pressure in the main system falls below 1,885 pounds per square inch, the hydraulic boost systems are switched off so that the main systems receive an adequate supply of hydraulic pressure, which is of vital importance to the flight control system:

The engine pods are under the fuselage, ensuring optimal airflow to the engines even at high angles of attack. *Sergey Chaikovsky*

First-level Systems:
• Aerodynamic control surfaces, hydraulic actuators tailerons, angle of attack limiting cylinder

Second-level Systems:
• All undercarriage components, engine air intake ramp control, speed brakes, APU cover flap

The hydraulic boost system supplies hydraulic actuators for the control surfaces and the angle of attack limiter. If the boost system fails or does not function properly, the general system takes over. The two NP-103A axial piston pumps, which are flange-mounted to the aircraft gearboxes, each have an output of up to 29 gal/min at an operating pressure of 3,045 pounds per square inch. A pressure relief valve in the system opens at 3,625 pounds per square inch and thus protects against an overload.

If both pumps fail at once, the ANS-58 emergency pump automatically engages, but it can also be turned on manually by a switch in the cockpit. It is located in the area of the gearbox and is powered by fuel delivered by the NP-96M pumps on the engines. The NP-96M also supplies the engine nozzle control cylinders. The ANS-58 produces 3,190 pounds of pressure, but it only supplies the hydraulic boost system's booster and the angle of attack limiter cylinder. To avoid gas in the hydraulic system, it is charged with nitrogen, which is located in the main undercarriage legs.

Flight Control System

The following describes the flight control system of the MiG-29 9.12, MiG-29S/SD/SE/SM and SMT, not that of the MiG-29M/K/M2, as this has an analogue/digital Fly-by-Wire system. The aircraft control system controls the rudders, ailerons, tailerons, leading edge flaps, flaps, and speed brakes. The control system consists of the actual SAU-451 control system (automatic flight control system), the SOS-3 (angle of attack limiter), the ARU automated regulator plus conventional rods, levers, and hydraulic components (cylinders, actuators, hydraulic boosters, and trim drives).

The SAU-451 system consists of one ARM-150M actuator per control channel, which are needed to dampen transitory vibrations in the control surfaces. Furthermore, an ARM-150APSU actuator in the longitudinal channel maintains longitudinal stability if yaw develops at high angles of attack when the leading edge flaps are extended. Two actuator drives serve as trim elements for the longitudinal and lateral control in all modes of operation (with the exception of damping). While the SAU-451 automatic control system is called an autopilot, in the actual sense it is not an automatic navigation system, meaning that one cannot fly from one point to the next preprogrammed point without pilot input. It is more of an automatic limiting system, which counters flight forces that arise and prevents or alerts the pilot to dangerous flight situations and maneuvers. These include:

• Ensuring damping while maintaining stability and controllability in the entire altitude and speed range
• Stabilization of the nominal angle of pitch and bank and of heading while under manual control
• Return to the horizontal from any flight attitude (emergency situation)
• Automatic pull-up from dangerously low altitude
• Automatic and manual control during landing approach to height of 150 feet
• Trimming of pitch and bank control during manual flight
• Stabilization of barometric altitude
• Indication of attitude on the artificial horizon

The SOS-3 angle of attack limiter is part of the SAU-451. Its roles are:

• Automatic deployment of the leading edge flaps
• Switching off of taileron differential deflection at angles of attack greater than 9°
• Activation of pitch kicker on reaching maximum allowable angle of attack (26°)

The automated regulator changes the control stick's operating load and the taileron deflection angle independent of altitude and speed. The taileron angle of deflection is greatest at low altitude and speed, while the force needed to operate the control stick is at its lowest. As speed increases, control stick resistance increases and the taileron angle of least. In the supersonic region the taileron deflection angle increases again, as in this speed range the effect on the control surfaces is not optimal, deflection becomes less and less. In the transonic and the immediate supersonic regions these values are at their maximum, control stick force is greatest, and the deflection angle increased.

Fuel System

The fuel system primarily serves to supply the engines and auxiliary power unit with fuel, but it also has other important functions, for example cooling the hydraulic drive system's lubricating oil from the AC generator and cooling air from the engine for the environmental system in the fuel-air cooler. There are seven internal fuel tanks, one in each wing (545 pounds each), between the engine compartments and between the vertical tails (Tank 3A, 255 pounds each) and three fuselage tanks one behind the other (Tank 1: 1,073 pounds, Tank 2: 1,437 pounds, and Tank 3: 2,990 pounds). In addition, a standard external tank can be carried under the fuselage (2,645 pounds) or a larger tank with a capacity of 3,790 pounds.

There are four different types of fuel pumps in the system, a DZN-80 booster and steering pump (impeller pump), five jet pumps (in Tanks 3, 3A, and wings; ejector principle), an electric centrifugal pump (in Tank 2; impeller pump) and four GTN-7 turbopumps (in Tanks 1, 2, and 3; turbine wheel pumps). The DZN-80 is flange-mounted on the gearbox and serves to power the turbopumps and jet pumps with fuel; the jet and turbopumps distribute and deliver fuel. The electric centrifugal pump is primarily there to supply the APU and engines with fuel during start-up, until the remaining pumps reach full output. Despite this, the electric centrifugal pump is never shut off during flight and ground operation. The pressurized external fuselage tank is the first fuel tank to be emptied. The German MiG-29s (9.12 variant) were modified to carry external wing tanks, each with a capacity of 1,900 pounds. All external tanks can be jettisoned once empty.

If the DZN-80 and the associated turbo- and jet pumps and the electric centrifugal pump fail, the engine-mounted DZN-78 feed pumps can suck sufficient fuel from the tanks to safely operate the engines, although in this mode the aircraft's performance range is limited. Reserve fuel capacity is 1,210 pounds and the pilot receives visual and acoustic warnings on reaching that level. The fuel gauge tells the pilot the quantity of fuel remaining, which tanks are empty, and range at the present performance profile and at economic flight. To prevent foaming or the formation of fuel vapor and thus the danger of an explosion, the tanks are pressurized with nitrogen or air drawn from the engine's low-pressure compressor. The 9.12 version has no emergency fuel jettison system, and air refueling capability was only added in the later versions (MiG-29K, SMT, M2). The aircraft is fueled from a central tank nozzle, which is located in the left main undercarriage bay, and it is also used for drainage of fuel on the ground for repair purposes. There are also drain plugs and valves to allow remaining fuel to drain from the tanks. If, in case of war, there are no fuelling installations or pressure refueling trucks available, fuel can be added manually using free-fall fueling openings on the upper sides of the wings. The external fuselage tank must be filled separately and fuel is added directly into the tank. Fueling is set on the PKUZO console next to the central tank nozzle, which also displays oil levels in the hydraulics, engines, and gearbox.

Engines and Accessory Gearbox System

At the end of the 1960s, work began on the engines which would power the next generation of fighter aircraft. Given this task were: the Klimov Engineering Company (OKB-117, headed by Klimov's successor Sergey Isotov, which mainly built turboshaft engines for Mil and Kamov helicopters), the Soyuz Engineering Company (OKB-300, headed by Sergey Tumanski), Arkhip Lyulka's engine design bureau, and the Permer Engine Design Bureau, headed by Pevel Solovyov (named after the city of Perm, where the design bureau was located). Lyulka's OKB built the AL-31F, which was installed in the Su-27, and Solovyov built the D-30F6 for the MiG-31. Both engines were too large for the small airframe of the MiG-29, however, and so a third engine had to be developed. Isotov's design was the RD-33, a twin-shaft turbofan design that produced about 18,210 pounds of thrust. Isotov also proposed a mechanically powered gearbox. Tumanski's R67-300 produced approximately 16,200 pounds of thrust with afterburner and was a three-shaft engine. Unlike Isotov's, Tumanski's gearbox was to be powered by pressurized air. After careful scrutiny by the MiG OKB and the TsIAM (Central Research and Development Institute for Engine Technology), Isotov's RD-33 was chosen. A deciding factor in this decision was that Tumanski's R67-300 was heavier than originally planned. The RD-33 and the gearbox (Isotov's was also chosen), together represented a weight savings of about 550 pounds. The RD-33 is a twin-shaft turbofan engine and has a bypass ratio of just under 0.5:1. The engine has four low-pressure stages and nine high-pressure stages, and the guide vanes of the first stage of the high-pressure compressor are adjustable. The combustion chamber is an annular design and it connects to a single-stage high- and low-pressure turbine. The RD-33 is equipped with an afterburner

RD-33 engine on an installation cart.

with variable nozzle and has hydro-mechanical engine control. This means that the most important control parameters are controlled by fuel pressure. BPR-88 and BPK-88 engine computers are also fitted. The APD-88 automatic start controls engine start on the ground and in the air (restart or precautionary start). If there is a total loss of electrical power to the engine, the entire engine, with the exception of the afterburner, continues to be safely controlled. Of course, during normal operation the engine is also monitored electronically, but in backup mode (purely hydro-mechanically) response is somewhat slower as the electronics react more quickly and more sensitively. The manufacturer Klimov offers a digital conversion for engine series with analogue control. This involves replacing the BPR-88 analogue computer and the BPK-88 with the BARK-88, and both engines can be converted within four hours. An anti-surge system (prevents pump surging) is integrated into the RD-33 that is one of the most reliable in the world; one can understand this if one has seen the MiG-29 perform the "Tail Slide Maneuver." In this maneuver the aircraft enters a 90-degree climb and gradually reduces power, until finally it stands for a few seconds on its own thrust stream. This maneuver (which, in addition to the MiG-29,

can only be flown by the Su-27 and its variants, with the exception of aircraft with thrust vector control) is proof of the RD-33's reliability, for usually in such attitudes the engine's vital air supply is simply cut off. This can result in a flameout, which is certainly not desirable, especially in such a maneuver. In addition to the RD-33's extremely stable gas dynamic, additional oxygen is injected into the engine when required, stabilizing the burn process in the combustion chamber.

Should the engine control linkages be damaged in combat, a spring mechanism places the RD-33 at maximum power. On the throttle lever are buttons for operating the speed brakes, the radio and releasing chaff and flares.

The RD-33 is attached to the airframe at four points. There are two thrust transmission bolts that are on a horizontal plane and represent installation attachment points, transmitting the thrust to the airframe. The engines are removed downwards and correspondingly installation is the reverse. It takes a team of three approximately three hours to complete an engine change, not including the subsequent test run. For the author it was always something special to sit in the cockpit as "brakeman" during a test run and handle the powerful RD-33. We were the only ones, other than the pilots, who could do this (with the exception of a few technical personnel authorized to carry out minor test runs). One can say that it was the best part of being an engine technician.

The purpose of the accessory gearbox (Russian designation KSA-2) was to produce pressure (3,045 pounds per square inch) for the hydraulic system and power (DC = 28V, AC = 115V 400 Hz). Flange-mounted to the gearbox are two hydraulic pumps, one AC and one DC generator, a fuel pump, and the starter and APU turbines. Furthermore, when the engines are started the flux is transmitted through the gearbox by cone gear wheels (during normal engine operation the larger of the two powers the gearbox). The fuel pump serves to power the turbopumps (fuel delivery pumps in the airframe tanks to the engines) and is mounted directly on the accessory gearbox and requires no power supply to operate, which makes it much less likely to fail than an electrically powered pump. The gearbox has its own closed oil circuit. The fire-extinguishing system ensures that any fires are extinguished, however the limited

quantity of fire-extinguishing agent means that just one fire can be fought. Sensors in the engine compartments and gearbox space signal the cockpit in the event of a fire.

In contrast to other gearbox designs, where each engine has a separate gearbox, here a single, compact accessory gearbox is installed. One might think that as a result there is no redundancy, however that is wrong. If the hydraulic pumps fail, fuel from the engines drives an emergency hydraulic pump. If the AC generator fails, the DC generator powers a converter (Russian designation: PTO) that produces alternating current. If the DV generator fails, the silver-zinc batteries supply the MiG-29 with direct current, which the PTO converts into alternating current. Under these conditions the batteries deliver power for the named systems for about twenty minutes. Should the fuel pump fail, the engine's own pumps draw sufficient fuel for the engines to run safely and stably.

There was a project called SMR-95, the object of which was to offer a modified RD-33 (RD-33N) to the South African Air Force for its Mirage F-1s and Super

Open engine and KSA (accessory gearbox) compartments atop the aircraft. The computer hatch is also open.

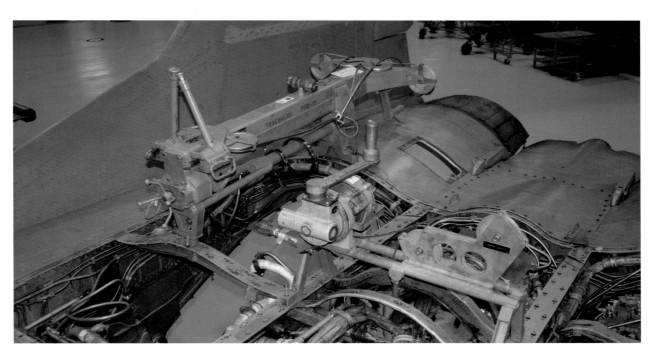

Engine and accessory gearbox crane in place.

The starboard engine compartment without engine.

RD-33 after removal, still suspended from the crane cables. It is not absolutely necessary to jack up the aircraft to remove an engine. In this special case work is also being carried out on the airframe. *Stefan Gawlista*

The KSA-2 accessory gearbox with angle drives removed. The latter form the mechanical linkage between the KSA-2 and RD-33.

The RD-33N with clearly longer jet pipe.

The KSA-53.

Cheetahs. The space available in the Mirage made it necessary to move the gearbox from the top of the RD-33 to the underside of the engine. As well, the accessory gearbox (KSA-53) was now installed on the RD-33. The jet pipe was considerably lengthened. The plan to convert the South African Mirage fleet came to nothing, however. This engine was later followed by the RD-93, which was a customized RD-33, also with the gearbox mounted beneath the engine. It was delivered to China for its FC-1 fighter aircraft (the JF-17 was an export version for Pakistan).

German Experience with the RD-33

The RD-33s in the German MiG-29s were Series 2 engines. Designed for a service life of 1,600 hours, the engines in the German MiGs together achieved approximately 72,000 operating hours. This was equal to about 1,000 hours per engine. While some logged as many as 1,300 hours, others had much less. In 1999 a German RD-33 became the first of its type anywhere in the world to reach the 1,000-hour mark. In terms of technical failures, the RD-33 Series 2 was considered one of the most dependable engines in the world. Some components and assemblies, however, sometimes proved subject to heavy wear. This was especially true of the jet nozzles, especially the nozzle petals and the associated connecting parts. This was attributed to the frequent power changes during aerial combat exercises, when the jet nozzles were working constantly. The high-pressure turbine blades also exhibited increased wear, which was also attributed to the previously named cause. This problem was addressed over time. There were several problematic incidents, however, which given the number of years the engine had been in use and its individual number of operating hours, reflected a high degree of reliability. These technical defects did not occur en masse, but on individual engines. What follows are the most noteworthy incidents.

During a training flight the fuel line of a pressure sensor on the engine broke and sprayed fuel into the engine compartment, but there was no fire. The entire German MiG-29 was grounded and not until all aircraft had been inspected and no further complaints found (checks were made to ensure the stressless installation of the fuel lines in question) was flying resumed. Examination revealed that a line attachment had broken, exposing the line to vibration, which it could not withstand. A modified, stronger anti-vibration bracket was installed and the problem never reappeared.

During a scheduled endoscopic check of an engine it was discovered that the combustion chamber had burned through. A crack near an injection nozzle radiated additional fuel and the undirected flame burned a hole in the combustion chamber. The high-pressure shaft was visible through the hole, and further use might have resulted in damage to the shaft, which could have had fatal results. All of the combustion chambers in the aircraft and the removed engines were endoscoped, however this too was an isolated incident.

A similar incident occurred when an engine was being

shut down. The pilot received warnings in the cockpit and the engine stopped. Once again the cause was a burn-through of the combustion chamber wall, which caused the high-pressure shaft to deform and seize. Once again all of the RD-33s had to be endoscoped. In this case the cause was a broken mounting for the injection nozzle ring and one of the tilted nozzles burned a hole in the combustion chamber wall. The ARM-OK evaluation system was retrofitted and it monitored a trend of temperature and pressure changes from flight to flight, and if there was a sudden considerable change an alarm was sounded. There was another combustion chamber burn-through in the last year of German MiG-29 operations. A flame burned through the combustion chamber and then all the way through the engine fairing. This was not discovered until post-landing checks on the ground, and in the air the pilot was unaware that anything was amiss.

These individual cases show that the RD-33 is a very well designed engine, and if there had been shortcomings in design or production the number of such incidents would have been much higher. Concerning repairs in Russia, however, a deterioration in the quality of the German engines was sometimes found in Laage.

In closing it can be said that the Russian manufacturer Chernishev acquired valuable long-term experience from the German MiG-29s. But it was not just the Russians who profited; employees of MTU were heard to say that the European consortium Eurojet also reaped considerable benefits for its EJ200 engine, which powers the Eurofighter.

The RD-33's lubrication system provides a clue to the state of the armaments industry in Russia in the 1990s. While the Germans were operating the MiG-29 there were occasional shortages of Russian IPM-10 lubricating oil. Flying operations sometimes had to be arranged so that no reduction in flying hours occurred because of normal oil consumption. The Russians claimed that a factory had been destroyed or damaged during the Chechen War then going on. The shortage was later overcome, but in Germany it left behind the fear that something similar might happen at any time. And so in 1998, the Bundeswehr began looking for an alternative oil in NATO supplies. One of the German MiG-29s was used to test a NATO oil. The complete lubrication system (engine, accessory gearbox, starter turbine, hydraulic drive system) was filled with the new oil, with which it was to undergo a 100-hour trial period. Oil samples were taken at regular intervals and sent to a laboratory for analysis. The filters associated with the assemblies were also checked. After reaching 1,200 hours the assemblies powered by the oil were removed and sent to the manufacturer in Russia for examination. There they were disassembled and found that the seals and bearings in the engines displayed increased wear and that additional carbonization had also formed in the bearings. Furthermore a type of oil carbon deposit was found in many places in the engine where the new oil came in contact with components. For this reason this oil was not used further in the German MiG-29s. In 2001, there were further shortages of IPM-10 and a French oil was used as a replacement, and it performed better than the oil previously tested.

In 2002, cracks were found in the accessory gearbox carrier frame, however there were no consequential damages. The Russian manufacturer developed a modified (stronger) frame and the original ones were replaced by unit engine mechanics.

After certain work on the engine, for example the replacement of certain engine assemblies or a complete engine change, it was necessary to test-run the engine. This could not be done in a maintenance hangar, and so such tests were simply carried out in the open. For this reason there were certain places on the airfield designated for engine runs (so-called run-up pads), which could only take place there.

A run-up pad was an area paved with concrete. Because the afterburner had to be engaged during a run-up, there also had to be somewhere to secure the aircraft. As the MiG-29 had no arrestor hook, which could be attached to an anchor, a jet blast deflector screen was set up on the run-up pad. This was attached to the main undercarriage legs with steel cables. When the jet blast blew against the deflector, the forces countered each other. To prevent the aircraft from moving with the jet blast deflector, the wheel brakes were engaged during the run-up. The braking pad also included a container in which there was regulating and measuring equipment. This was the operator's "office," who was also in charge of the run-up, monitoring the engine during the run-up, and making precise adjustments if necessary. In the beginning the container was neither heated nor air-conditioned, which made it very uncomfortable in winter and summer. Later an electric heater was added. To spare the aircraft's batteries during engine start, a mobile diesel generator was generally used to start the engines. It was shut down as soon as the aircraft produced its own alternating voltage. A light standard was set up for night operations.

The most uncomfortable place during an engine run-up was that of the safety lookout. During the entire test he was responsible for keeping an eye on the aircraft and especially the engine area. For he had to immediately deal with leaks, fires, or jet nozzle ejections himself or report them to the operator and the man operating the brakes. All three were

RD-33 Technical Specification	
Length	13.87 feet
Diameter	4.10 feet
Weight	2,315 pounds
Air Flow	170 pounds/second
Thrust at Idle	405 pounds
Maximum Thrust	11,105 pounds
Maximum Afterburner	18,300 pounds
Fuel Consumption Idle	838 pounds/hour
Fuel Consumption Maximum	8,444 pounds/hour
Afterburner maximum	36,597 pounds/hour
Maximum RPM NDV	11,000 rpm
Maximum RPM HDV	15,500 rpm
Maximum Pressure Ratio	22:1

connected by voice communications. The brake operator sat in the cockpit and operated the engines and necessary aircraft systems. Certain work was carried out with the engines running, which especially in winter could be very uncomfortable. Delicate work in cold weather was made difficult by stiff fingers. The personnel had to be particularly attentive when rain was expected. If cables had to be attached to the onboard computer, the associated hatch had to be opened and it was on the upper surface of the airframe. If rain entered there it could damage the computer. The time of day was a further limiting factor, for after a certain time in the evening no further run-ups were allowed (with the exception of very short stages), for the very loud engines could be heard clearly in the nearby, populated areas. It was for this reason that a run-up hangar was built. Engine run-ups could be carried out there without regard to time of day or weather. The hangar's exhaust channel was built in such a way as to have a sound dampening effect.

JG 73's run-up hangar was placed in service in 1999. Lastly it is observed that during the whole time that *JG 73* operated the MiG-29, there was not a single accident during an engine run-up (with the exception of a fall from a ladder). This speaks to the high level of professionalism demonstrated by the military and civilian personnel of *JG 73*. Use of the sound protection hangar was especially welcomed by the safety lookouts. They were now only in the hangar from engine start to idle, at higher rpm they had to leave the hangar because the effects of acoustic pressure on the body were too great. On the braking pad these were not restrained by walls and were, though difficult, somewhat more bearable.

If the test was just a leak check, during which the engine could not exceed 85% of maximum rpm, it could also be carried out in an aircraft shelter. Many run-ups, which were primarily short leak checks, were also carried out on the flight line. During peacetime engine performance was restricted by lowering the turbine intake temperature. This resulted in longer engine life. This reduction was designated "training regime," and only the intake temperature was lowered. In the early years this required the onboard computer to be removed, recalibrated, and installed again, with a subsequent engine run-up. To achieve "normal" full performance, the above process was carried out in reverse. Later the UR-Cha-7 plug was procured, which was inserted when a computer was set at normal, resulting in the "training regime." No engine run-up was required. In the event of war the "RPT regime" could be set which gave the RD-33 its maximum performance. This reduced engine life considerably, however.

JG 73's "burner pad" prior to construction of the noise reduction hangar. All major test runs were carried out here in the open. In the left background is the jet blast deflector, to the left a concrete exhaust deflector, and in the left foreground the container in which the operator and his equipment were housed (concealed here by a ground equipment container).

Evening test run on the burner pad with maximum afterburner. One can imagine the ear-shattering noise.

MiG-29 29+20 in the noise protection hangar.

Impressive flame produced by the turbostarter. In this case the flame was only so large because, after depreservation, the first hot start injection took place with the injection of additional oxygen and the remaining preservative oil was burned with it. Such a large flame was not a feature of a normal engine start.

Smaller test runs (for example leak test runs) could be carried out in the shelter as shown here, however the engines could not exceed 85% of maximum rpm.

Test run on the flight line. Leak checks (especially of the airframe fuel system) could also be carried out here. *Stefan Gawlista*

Engine run-up at night on the flight line.

Pneumatic System

The Soviet designers took an uncomplicated path in creating the aircraft's pneumatic system, but the resulting system was extremely reliable. This is also the reason why important systems in the aircraft function on the basis of this system. These include the mainwheel brakes, operation and sealing of the cockpit canopy, release and jettisoning of the braking chute, opening and closing of the main fuel shut-off valve, low-pressure ventilation of the hydraulic system and low-pressure ventilation of the cooling system housing, the waveguide, and the radar equipment. If the main system fails, the emergency system lowers the undercarriage and operates the mainwheel brakes only. It is physically separated from the main system and thus provides high reliability. Nitrogen can be used as a medium and is fed into several containers at 2,175 pounds per square inch of pressure. The filling point is located in the port main undercarriage bay, along with the manometer that indicates system pressure. In the cockpit there is a combined indicator which displays hydraulic pressure as well as pressure for the main and back-up compressed air

systems. A certain air pressure must be maintained in the radar compartment to prevent flashover in the radar waveguides. In addition to actual braking, the brake system ensures that the wheels do not become locked during braking (ABS) and that during turns while taxiing only the wheel on the interior of the turn is braked, enabling a smaller turning circle (neither is active when the back-up system is functioning.

The braking parachute system has its own compressed air container and is thus fully independent, although it is filled from a common point. There are two buttons in the cockpit, one to release the barking chute, the other to jettison it. The parachute can be deployed at speeds up to 192 miles per hour, at higher speeds a sheer bolt separates and the chute is set free. The braking chute has an area of 183 square feet. Landing roll without the parachute is 3,117 feet, and with the chute this is shortened to 2,133 feet. Obviously the chute can be reused.

A rather used-looking Iranian MiG with deployed braking chute. As a rule the chute was jettisoned at specific places where it was recovered by ground personnel. *Babak Taghvaee*

Undercarriage

The MiG-29's undercarriage consists of a twin-wheel nose undercarriage and mainwheel undercarriage legs with single wheels. The air pressure in the tires is somewhat lower than usual, allowing the aircraft to also operate from prepared strips. The undercarriage legs are filled with a nitrogen-hydraulic fluid medium to absorb the impact of landing and other taxiing loads. In normal mode the nosewheel can pivot +/- 31 degrees while taxiing and +/- 8 degrees during takeoff and landing. A stone deflector on the nosewheel undercarriage prevents debris from being thrown into the engine intakes during takeoff and landing. The main undercarriage legs are not mounted at right angles to the aircraft's longitudinal axis, but are inclined forward slightly. This arrangement transmits the shock of landing straight into the main undercarriage legs, as they are vertical to the effect of the landing forces.

All of the undercarriage system's wheels have multiple disc brakes and are operated pneumatically. If the main pneumatic system is not functioning properly, braking can be achieved using an emergency braking system with an independent pneumatic system, and braking of the nosewheel can even be shut off completely. Should the brakes overheat during braking, tin bezels melt, revealing small holes so that the increased air pressure in the tires can drop quickly, preventing the tires from blowing. Melted tin bezels are detected during the following routine inspection and necessary repairs to the undercarriage are initiated. Undercarriage lowering and retraction is normally carried out hydraulically. If the system fails, a pneumatic back-up system takes over. The pilot pulls a lever in the cockpit and the nosewheel undercarriage is lowered pneumatically. The main undercarriage is simply unlocked and lowers by its own weight. The airstream forces the undercarriage down further (as it extends rearward), where it then locks. The tires have small depressions that serve as wear markings. When they are no longer visible it is time to change the tires.

The original nosewheel undercarriage of the first MiG-29 prototype 901. Note the large stone deflector behind the wheels. Right: The modified nosewheel undercarriage of the production aircraft. It has clearly been moved to the rear and has a modified stone deflector.

Radar

To be able to successfully engage the new generation of American combat aircraft (which then included the B-1 bomber), a completely new radar was needed for the new Soviet fighter aircraft. Operational studies by the Americans envisaged low-level penetration missions into enemy territory at high subsonic speeds. The MiG-23's radar was ill suited to meet this type of threat. The new radar was first tested in the seventh prototype MiG-29 (918), which made its first flight in 1980. Designated N-019, it was the first Soviet radar to have look down/shoot down capabilities, which meant that it was capable of detecting and engaging fast, low-flying targets against background clutter. The N-019 is a pulse-Doppler radar and has a range against fighter-size targets (radar reflective area of 32 square feet) of approximately fifty miles and can lock on from about 35 miles. It can track ten targets simultaneously but can engage only one at a time. The radar selects the closest target with the highest closing speed. The pilot can, however, select another target using controls on the control stick.

When the USA had the opportunity to test the MiG-29 after the fall of the Soviet Union, it was astonished by the radar's resistance to jamming. The N-019 weighs 770 pounds, and is made by the Phazotron Company.

Should the MiG-29 come under missile attack, the pilot can use flares and chaff to deploy the weapon. The chaff/flare dispensers are incorporated in the forward vertical tail roots. A total of sixty chaff/flare cartridges are carried, and these can be deployed by the pilot with the push of a button.

Radar Warning System

The MiG-29 has a radar warning system to alert the pilot when his aircraft is illuminated by an enemy radar. The system's receiver is installed so that it provides 360-degree coverage.

The radar antenna complex of the NO-19.

The indicator in the cockpit provides precise information about the general direction and hemisphere of the threat and also the type of radar (fighter aircraft, short-, medium-, or long-range air defense positions or AWACS), direction of beams, and sometimes even the type of aircraft. The pilot is also informed whether the aircraft is being constantly illuminated or only occasionally, and finally if the enemy radar is locked on and thus at the point of firing a guided missile. If this is the case, the indicator around the aircraft silhouette flashes red and a loud acoustic signal alerts the pilot.

Optronics

In addition to the radar, there is an additional tracking system, called the IRST (Infra Red Search and Track) and a laser range finder. The IRST is a passive sensor, as it produces no radiation, instead receiving heat radiation (infrared light) from hostile targets (whether exhaust gases or airframe heating). The enemy is unaware that he has

been detected and begins no countermeasures. The radar, the IRST and the helmet-mounted sight (described later) always work together, which means if the IRST loses its target in cloud the radar automatically switches on so that the target contact is not lost. The helmet-mounted sight works as follows: when the pilot turns his head the missile seeker heads turn the same way, as do the radar antenna and the ORST. The search method that allows the aircraft to remain undetected for as long as possible is always used (IRST and radar, as the helmet-mounted sight has to be manually selected by the pilot). A pilot immediately betrays his position by switching on his radar, as the enemy aircraft has a radar warning receiver and can identify the position of the transmitter. The IRST's maximum range in search mode is nine miles and tracking range is about seven miles. Also built into the IRST is a laser range finder, which is mainly used to precisely determine the range to the target for accurate use of the cannon, as the radar is too imprecise for this purpose. The improved accuracy means that fewer cannon rounds have to be fired. The range of the laser range finder is up to four miles. The range indications from the optical system are based on good weather conditions.

The optic package of the IRST/LR in installed condition.

Helmet-Mounted Sight

The helmet-mounted sight is used to guide R-73 short-range air-to-air missiles in aerial combat, to attack targets off boresight (up to 60 degrees with the R-73). This has the advantage that so much time does not have to be spent aligning the aircraft with the target; the pilot simply looks at the target and the missile's seeker head points where he is looking.

On the helmet there are diodes that emit a beam of light and are broken and redirected by glass prisms (located in the base of the Head-Up Display). This enables the weapons computer to determine exactly where the pilot is looking and consequently where the missile has to fly. During joint exercises with the German MiG-29s in the USA the superiority of this system came as such a surprise that the design of helmet-mounted sights received much higher priority in the western nations. For in close air combat they were simply inferior to the MiG-29 armed with the R-73. The sight is, however, a very simple design. The primary objective of the Soviet designers was the most effective possible engagement of targets. A small green circle is produced on the helmet-mounted sight's visor shield. This then serves as the targeting circle for the pilot, with which to guide the R-73 to its target.

This does not require the large and heavy displays of other expensively designed helmets. The success achieved by German pilots in exercises confirmed this approach–and they did so twenty to twenty-five years after the helmet-mounted sight was developed.

In the Bundeswehr the pilots later used the HGU-55 helmet, on which was fitted the Russian helmet-mounted sight.

Revised helmet-mounted sight on a
likewise new pilot helmet.

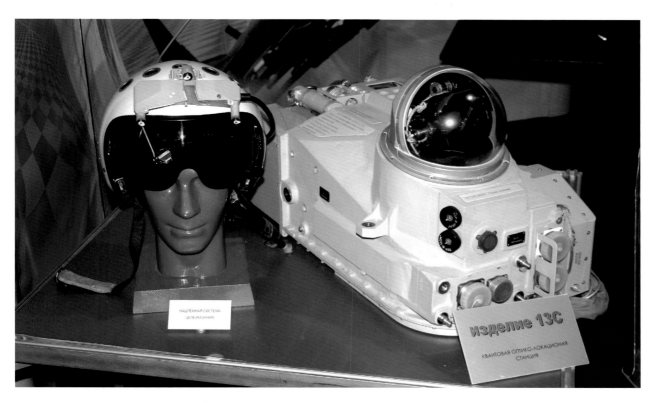

The terror of the MiG-29's opponents: the IRST/LR and Sch-7A helmet with helmet-mounted sight.

The older Sch-5A helmet could also be fitted with the helmet-mounted sight. The helmet sight in detail: located in the center, the actual deployed sight. On the left and right extremities and above, the laser diodes for the rotation prism and the projection lens above the visor.

Electrical System

The MiG-29's electrical system is made up of three different systems: a DC system, an AC system, and a battery power system. The DC system delivers 28.5 V, 400 A, and 12 kW. The main provider is the GSR-ST-12/40A generator, which is installed on the accessory gearbox but is cooled by an air scoop in the outer skin of the MiG-29. The BRZ-1 regulator and overload protection device delivers consistent current values. It also prevents a power surge or short circuit from damaging the system. Should the DC generator cease to function, the DC batteries automatically engage. These ensure a DC power supply of 27.5 V for between fifteen and twenty minutes. Non flight-relevant systems such as the radar, the IRST/LR, the radar warning receiver, and the radio navigation system are separated from the battery supply, however. The pilot is alerted to the failure of the DC generator acoustically and by the Ekran indicator. The batteries can also be used for autonomous ground operation, for example to start the engines, operate the GTDE-117 auxiliary power unit (which provides a supply of hydraulic pressure, AC and DC power, or use of the air conditioning system) or simply to supply general power.

The silver-zinc batteries are not charged during flight and this has to happen while the aircraft is on the ground. Another disadvantage is that capacity drops sharply at temperatures below 41 degrees F. To deal with this, the batteries in the MiG are heated or the aircraft is connected to external power on the ground. The AC power supply is delivered by a GT-30 NSh 412 AC generator and a PTO-1000/1500 generator transformer. The AC generator is flange-mounted to the accessory gearbox and consequently turns at different speeds. To nevertheless achieve a constant frequency of 400 Hz, a GP-21 hydro-mechanical hydraulic drive is interposed between the generator and accessory gearbox. The generator produces 36 V, 117 V, and 202 V, each at 400 Hz, and an output of 30 kVA. It is cooled by the oil system of the GP-21. If the AC generator fails to deliver the required values, the PTO transformer takes over the supply of AC. It is powered by direct current and with

The KSA-2 with brown oil tank, left beside it the alternating current generator with coupled GP-21 hydraulic drive, installed behind it the turbo starter, and above it the black DC generator.

The cockpit energy center (circuit breaker box) directly behind the headrest of the K-36 ejection seat. *Stefan Gawlista*

transformers produces the necessary AC supply, but only for flight-relevant systems. The pilot can separate the AC generator from the GP-21 from the cockpit if it becomes necessary (for example to protect the hydraulic drive from damage) and he receives a corresponding warning indication. During ground operations both the AC and DC supplies can be provided by ground equipment. The necessary connections are in the port undercarriage bay and the wing root. Circuit breakers located in a console behind the ejection seat protect the electrical system. To protect the equipment and the ground personnel from damage or injury, some circuit breakers are pulled on the ground to prevent inadvertent operation of the affected systems.

Navigation

The navigation system is used to determine the aircraft's attitude in space and its position. This can be accomplished using systems on board the aircraft or by information transmitted from ground systems. It also delivers information to the flight control system, the cockpit instrumentation, and the Head-up Display and can guide the MiG-29 to a preprogrammed airfield, including automatic landing approach to a height of about 150 feet above touchdown. Finally the navigation system also provides the weapons system with speed data. The fuel-range indicator also receives its data from the system.

The navigation system consists of the short-range navigation system (RSBN for Russian versions), the air data system, and the associated conversion and computer systems. In the RSBN system, stationary radio stations on the ground transmit signals that are processed by the MiG-29. The RSBN enables a route of flight to be preprogrammed, as well as the landing approach at a selected airfield (provided it is equipped with an instrument landing system). Since the MiG-29M and K (9.15 and 9.31), there have been better systems, such as satellite and laser-gyro systems on board. A special navigation system for marine operations is installed in the K versions (carrier-based). The antennas for the RSBN form a trident on the rear edge of the vertical stabilizers and there is a rectangular antenna beneath the nose. A western ILS system was installed in the German MiGs. This can be identified by the small yellow triangular antennas on the fuselage spine aft of the cockpit and under the fuselage nose.

Air Data System

This system is supplied with data by the main and secondary pitot tubes, temperature sensors, and angle of attack and yaw vanes (all of the named items are heated during flight to prevent the formation of ice and loss of data). If the main pitot tube fails, the pilot can switch to the secondary pitot tube. These air pressure values are converted into electrical signals and fed to the cockpit instruments, the Head-up Display, the navigation, flight control and weapons systems, the engines, the automatic ejection controls, the flight recorder, and the cockpit pneumatic system. On the MiG-29M and M2 as well as the K variants (9.31/9.41) there is a third pitot tube beneath the fuselage. The main pitot tube of all MiG-29s is located at the tip of the radome, the secondary pitot tube on the right side of the fuselage forward of the windscreen. The angle of attack and yaw vanes are beneath the fuselage nose on the right and left sides, and the MiG-29OVT has additional angle of attack vanes. The temperature sensors are located on the fuselage nose and the engine temperature sensors are installed on the vertical tail surfaces.

Radio Navigation

The pieces of equipment that make up the radio navigation system are the radio compass, marker beacon receiver, radio altimeter (with associated cockpit indicators), and a transponder. The ARK-19 radio compass measures the angle of ground stations and compares them to the aircraft's longitudinal axis, from which the course is calculated. The signals transmitted by the ground station are received by the antennas on the fuselage spine. Reception range is dependent on the MiG's altitude and the power of the radio beacon. The A-037 radio altimeter with transmitting and receiving antennas is installed in the fuselage nose. The purpose of the radio altimeter is to accurately measure the aircraft's height above ground up to an altitude of 3,280 feet, for the barometric altimeter is too imprecise with differing barometric pressures and terrain heights. A minimum height can be set on the radio altimeter, and an alarm is sounded if the aircraft goes below this height.

The A-611 marker beacon receiver helps locate friendly airfields. The airfield beacons have an inner and an outer circle, which on passing this area transmit an

acoustic warning in the pilot's headset. The SO-69 transponder of an aircraft flying in this zone transmits signals to air traffic control. This information includes the aircraft identification, altitude, and speed. These signals appear on the ATC radar screens, ensuring the safe and clear coordination and control of the aircraft in the air. In time of war operations can also be supported from the ground in this way. The transponder antennas are beneath the fuselage nose, the port wing root, and the trailing edge of the starboard vertical tail.

Radio Communication

The radio communications system consists of the VHF radio, intercom system, and the emergency radio set. The R-862 VHF system is used for air-ground communications. It transmits in the meter or decimeter range in the 100 to 400 MHz frequency range with 2,000 fixed channels in this range and 7,200 in a wider range. Operating range is again dependent on altitude, about seventy miles at 3,000 feet, and approximately 215 miles at 30,000 feet. The VHF radio antenna is located beneath the cap of the starboard vertical tail. The SPU-9 intercom system allows the pilot to transmit over the VHF radio, receive signals from the radio beacon receiver, and acoustic reports from internal systems. These include warnings by voice systems, the radar warning receiver, the optical targeting complex when it locks onto a target, and signals from ground stations via data link. On the ground the SPU system also allows the pilot to communicate with ground personnel. A cable is plugged into a box under the fuselage nose (MiG-29UB) or in the main undercarriage bay (single-seaters), allowing voice communications between the pilot and the ground personnel. This is also used when there is a technician working in the cockpit, as during engine run-ups, for example. In the MiG-29UB the SPU system allows the instructor to communicate with the pupil. The R-855UM emergency radio is used to locate the crew in the event of an ejection or a forced landing by the aircraft. It allows the pilot to communicate with the crews of rescue helicopters or search aircraft. It has a range of up to thirty miles provided the rescue aircraft is flying at an altitude of at least 9,000 feet. The radio can also serve as a radio beacon and in this role has a range of up to forty miles. The batteries have an operating life of twenty-four, to a maximum of fifty-five hours, depending on operating mode. The emergency radio is part of the NASS-7 survival kit in the seat pan of the ejection seat. It is contained in a self-inflating buoy-like housing. This is made of orange material to ease location and is buoyant. The antenna sits up and the battery delivers power to the radio. The pilot can remove the emergency radio for transportation on land.

Air Conditioning and Pressurization System

The air conditioning and pressurization system regulates the temperature and pressure in the cockpit, the cooling of the avionics and cannon, supplies the ventilation suit and the anti-g system, and prevents fogging of the canopy. Air is drawn from the area of the high pressure compressor, which compression has heated to 930 to 1,020 degrees F. This is reduced to about 390 degrees by air-to-air cooling. Then the air is dried and fed to the turbo-cooler, where it is finally cooled to 40 degrees F. The desired cockpit temperature is achieved by mixing it with air that is about 390 degrees hotter. Before the air finally flows into the cockpit, the air pressure is regulated by automatic pressure regulators. The pilot can set a temperature in the range from 60 to 77 degrees F, which is then automatically maintained. He can select three climate control modes: cooling, heating, or automatic. Warm air is blown onto the canopy. The pilot can also manually select a higher setting. The air conditioning system also provides cooling for the avionics, although the temperature is far lower than that in the cockpit. Pipes carry the cold air to or into the avionics blocks. If the cooling fails, the overheating equipment shuts off to prevent damage and an indicator informs the pilot. The radar is also cooled by a coolant (alcohol mixture). This is a closed system that contains 2.6 gallons of this coolant. If the upper limit of 159 degrees is exceeded or the pressure in the cooling system is too high or low, the radar shuts off. Furthermore blocks in the radar, the IFF, and other HF blocks are pressurized, as is the radar coolant reservoir. The air conditioning system is located in the starboard leading edge root extension and is accessible by large hatches for maintenance.

Oxygen System

The oxygen system provides the pilot with breathing air during flight, an emergency supply in case of ejection or failure of the primary oxygen system, and starter support for the engines and turbostarter. Gaseous oxygen is contained in pressure cylinders that are in completely separate systems. The main system provides the pilot with the required oxygen in the hermetically sealed cockpit in all flight regimes and altitudes. Oxygen is delivered by the oxygen mask, which is connected to the oxygen system by the ORK quick-separation bar (attached to the ejection seat). Four operating modes are possible:

- Mixture (0 – 6,500 feet, pure environmental air, enriched with oxygen from 6,500 to 26,250 feet)
- Pure oxygen breathing (26,250 to 39,000 feet)
- Overpressure breathing
- Emergency supply and helmet ventilation

The quantity of gaseous oxygen under pressure in the main system is 732 cubic inches (three cylinders each holding 243 cubic inches), which at normal pressure would give about 55 cubic feet of oxygen (in the single-seater—figures for the MiG-29UB are 1,585 cubic inches under pressure, 119 cubic feet under normal pressure). The indicator in the cockpit shows the pilot actual cockpit altitude, oxygen remaining, lung function, and the differential pressure compared to the surrounding atmospheric pressure. At altitudes above 39,370 feet and/or reaching 15% remaining oxygen, the Ekran gives a report and the pilot receives a voice advisory. If malfunctions occur, he can override the system. The emergency oxygen supply is held in a forty-two-cubic-inch cylinder that is located in the seat pan of the K-36 ejection seat. It is activated either manually, by pulling a handle on the right side of the seat, or automatically in the event of ejection.

The engine oxygen system is used for an engine restart in flight if one or both engines fail. As well, as a precautionary measure oxygen is sprayed into the combustion chambers when the cannon or missiles are used, to prevent gases from interfering with or extinguishing combustion in the engine. Oxygen is also fed if the engine monitoring system detects compressor surging.

A Russian autonomous oxygen system made by Zvezda was first tested on a MiG-29M2 in 2004. This system requires no oxygen cylinders, as it extracts the necessary oxygen from compressed air drawn from the engine compressor. This air is both dehumidified and cleaned—even chemically, bacterially, or nuclear contaminated atmosphere can be flown through. The main advantage of this system compared to the earlier cylinder system is obviously its much greater operational endurance, which is no longer limited by the amount of oxygen that is carried. Another advantage is its reduced weight (70.5 pounds) and space required. During intensive flying, constant monitoring of the amount of oxygen remaining and top-up are no longer required, which further reduces maintenance costs.

The system is designed to provide sufficient oxygen for two pilots to an altitude of 65,600 feet. At present it is used in the MiG-35 and Indian MiG-29K. The Russian air force command would like to see the system in all its MiG-29s and Su-27s. Simultaneous with this development the emergency oxygen system was also changed. Originally there was an oxygen bottle in the seat pan. This was replaced with a chemical oxygen generator, making the system virtually maintenance free.

Pilot Equipment

As a rule, MiG-29 pilots use the Sch-7A helmet with the KM-35 oxygen mask. The helmet provides protection during ejection and to accept the helmet-mounted sight, the oxygen mask and headset as well as the sun shield. The oxygen mask supplies the pilot with the required oxygen during a variety of maneuvers. In addition to supplying the pilot with oxygen during ejection, the system even enables him to breathe underwater for five minutes! The German Air Force MiG-29 pilots used the HGU-55 NATO helmet that was fitted with the necessary adapters for connection to the MiG's radio system.

Appropriate clothing is required to enable the pilot to retain his maximum performance abilities even at high g-forces. For the stronger these forces become during air combat maneuvers, the more a considerable portion of the pilot's blood collects in the his legs (under positive g-forces). The result ranges from tunnel vision to loss of consciousness, as the brain no longer receives an adequate blood supply. To prevent the blood from collecting in the legs, either anti-g pants (PPK-3) or a complete anti-g suit

(WKK-15) is used. Both have air chambers that are connected to the cockpit pressurization system or the ORK bar by tubes. Air is pumped into the pockets to exert pressure on the legs and thorax. This keeps blood in the body core. This is supported by deep breathing and tensing of the abdominal muscles by the pilot. If missions above 39,000 to 69,000 feet are expected, the pressure suit is used, while the anti-g pants are used up to an altitude of 36,000 feet. The suit, however, makes the pilot better able to withstand high g-forces at all altitudes.

A new suit with a liquid filling (the so-called dragonfly suit) was tested successfully (see the chapter on German MiGs).

K-36 Ejection Seat

The K-36 is a zero-zero seat, which means that the pilot can safely leave the aircraft and have his parachute fully deploy at a speed of zero miles per hour and an altitude of zero feet. On the other side of the scale the pilot can eject at a speed of up to 870 miles per hour up to the maximum service ceiling. For this eventuality the seat cushion contains an emergency oxygen system, emergency rations, a life raft, and other means with which to survive in the wild for some time. To help locate

Sch-7A helmet oxygen mask and lowered sun visor.

WKK-15 anti-g
suit.

the downed pilot, it also has an emergency radio, which can be used for voice communication or as a radio beacon. Range varies between ten and forty miles and is dependant on the altitude of the search aircraft.

The K-36DM firing sequence is electric, but there is a mechanical backup. This is partly responsible for its extremely high success rate of 97%. The seat weighs about 165 pounds and is thus considerably lighter than earlier ejection seats and comparable to seats made by the British manufacturer Martin Baker.

The ejection process begins with the pulling of the handgrips between the pilot's legs. Unlike western jets, where the canopy glass is blown out, on the MiG-29 the canopy is unlocked pyrotechnically and raised. This of course does not work on the ground; there the rising seat mechanically lifts the canopy and moves it out of the way. There is a manual emergency opening for opening the canopy from the outside. In the air the canopy pulls a line as it flies away, which unlocks the ejection seat for firing.

Before the pilot can safely leave the aircraft, his limbs must first be restrained to avoid injury. The pilot's legs are lifted up. The arm restriction system is activated. Then the waist straps are automatically tightened. The pilot is thus locked in his seat. If this locking into position did not happen (all of this takes place in fractions of a second) the pilot could possibly sustain very serious injuries, as his feet would still be on the pedals beneath the instrument panel. The same could be said of the arms, which would flail about during ejection.

Two telescopic booms (approximately 5.25 feet), which are next to the headrest and deploy rearward, each have a small stabilizing parachute at their ends. As the seat falls the airflow causes them to turn in opposite directions. This design brings the seat to a stable attitude as it falls, namely with the front of the body facing downward. The K-36 in its various versions is used in

the Su-22/-24/-25/-27 (and their versions), the MiG-31, and the Tu-160 strategic bomber and was even used by the Soviet Buran space shuttle and the Yak-41 VTOL fighter. The latest version is the K-36D-3.5, which is used in the newer K and M versions and the MiG-35. This seat has a reduced weight of 227 pounds and it is at least as capable as its predecessor. Operational life is 5,000 hours or thirty years.

Cockpit Instrumentation

The MiG-29's primary indicators were analogue indicators and vertical-display instruments combined with the SEI-31 Head-up Display and the display screen (cathode ray principle) in the upper right of the instrument panel. The most important flight instruments (barometric altimeter, airspeed indicator, vertical speed indicator/turn and slip indicator, course indicator, and flight direction indicator) are framed in white for quicker perception by the pilot. The advantage of analogue indicators is that when looking at the instrument a pointer is in a certain area of the indicator scale and the eye immediately recognizes whether the parameter is in a critical or a normal region. Digital instruments often display a value as a number, which the brain must first process. For this reason, much work has been done in this area with symbols and different colors (green, yellow, red, blue). The advantage of digital indicators, on the other hand, is that significantly more parameters and various displays can be shown. These screens are also capable of controlling systems in flight and during maintenance work on the ground.

Warning and Information Systems

There are four different systems that inform the pilot during flight or technical personnel on the ground about dangerous situations or certain operating conditions. The first and most simple is the master caution light. It is a red warning light directly to the left of the Head-up Display (HUD) and thus in the pilot's direct field of vision. It begins to flash as soon as aircraft systems near a dangerous condition. Together with other warning systems, the pilot is able to gain an overall view and localize the source of the problem.

K-36DM Specification	
Weight	265 pounds
Ejection superelevation	approx. 42 feet
Number of rocket stages	2
Second stage thrust	7,418 pounds
Maximum acceleration on ejection	18 – 20 g
Duration of maximum acceleration	0.12 – 0.15 seconds
Seat height adjustment	0 – 6.3 inches
Parachute area	646 square feet

K-36 ejection seat installed in the MiG-29. The tubes next to the headrest contain the stabilizing parachutes.

K-36D-3.5
ejection seat.

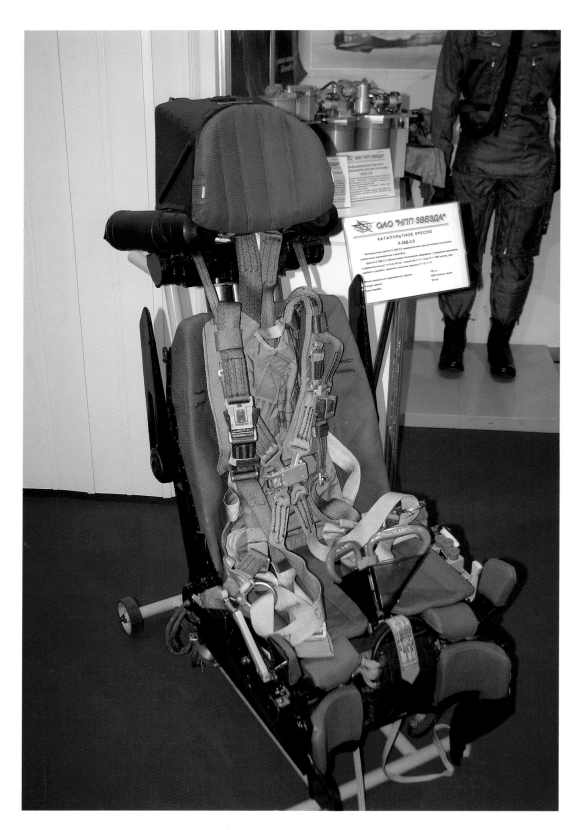

This is a function of the EKRAN (systems damage display) panel.

It is located at the right edge of the instrument panel. Text is burned into a metal-covered roll of analogue film. Up to 194 prepared warning texts are available for the MiG-29. These are permanently programmed and appear on the indicator device, for example "Fire LH Eng" (fire left engine). Only the most important indication at the moment appears in the indicator window. If other indications are received by the EKRAN, the message TURN appears and the pilot or technician can scroll through the list by pressing a button. The EKRAN roll is removed after each flight for evaluation and a new one is installed. Up to sixty-four reports can be shown on each roll. If the EKRAN itself malfunctions, the indicator field ERROR appears.

Another system available to pilots and technicians displays text indicator fields. These are combined into a large table that is located to the right of the EKRAN panel, while individual light indicators are arranged on the left and right switch consoles. Indicator fields are displayed in different colors, for example green for systems that are engaged, yellow for warning signals and red for dangerous conditions. As soon as an indicator field comes on, the master caution light starts to flash. The flashing can be changed to a steady light by pressing on the same. The MiG-29's last warning system is the voice warning system. As a female voice is used (which according to psychologists has a calming effect on pilots), the Soviets jokingly call the system Natasha and the Germans Rita. Up to forty-six permanently recorded warnings (magnetic tape) can be played over the pilot's headset in his helmet or through the sound protection helmet of the ground technician. In addition to the actual warning, the messages also contain brief recommendations. In case of engine fires, accessory gearbox fires or fuel interruption, these voice warnings are automatically transmitted to the ground by radio.

The flight recorder is also part of the information system. It records parameters (just under 500) concerning aircraft technical information, pilot actions, and aircraft flight data (for example, angle of attack, speed, altitude, etc.) on a magnetic tape. After each flight the data is analyzed and deviations checked. This reveals if technical systems are malfunctioning or showing a tendency to do so. It also reveals if the pilot has flown outside the allowable limits. If there is an accident, depending on its condition the flight recorder can help determine the cause. For this reason it is kept in a very durable container. The manufacturer guarantees that about 95% of the data

will be usable if the recorder spends a maximum of two days in water, three days in salt water, fifteen minutes at temperatures up to 1,800 degrees F or 10 ms of acceleration up to 32,150 feet per second squared. The container is painted orange for ease of location after a crash. The flight data recorder is either switched on manually in the cockpit, or automatically if certain conditions exist which suggest that major repairs will be required (for example, engine rpm greater than 85% or unloading of a main undercarriage leg or landing flap).

R-73 (above) and R-77 (below) AAMs on the folded wing segment of the MiG-29K 9.31. Note the grid tail fins of the R-77. *Stefan Gawlista*

Chapter 7

Armament

R-73 AA-11 Archer

The emergence of the new generation of Soviet fighters exemplified by the MiG-29 and Su-27 was accompanied by the creation of a completely new generation of air-to-air missiles. These were the medium- and short-range R-27 AA-10 Alamo and the R-73 AA-11 Archer short-range dogfighting missile. Introduced in the mid-1980s, this missile still dominates the short-range missile sector worldwide. It was designed to engage hard-maneuvering targets at short range, but it can also be used against ground targets in a secondary role. The infrared seeker head has a 45-degree angle of view and in conjunction with the helmet-mounted sight it can see and engage targets up to 45 degrees off the missile's centerline (see Helmet-Mounted Sight).

The missile can engage targets from sixty-five feet to 65,000 feet at speeds up to 1,550 miles per hour. The missile is capable of locking on, even if the target is pulling up to 12 g. Its outstanding feature is its control system, which combines aerodynamic control surfaces with thrust vectoring. Because of this the R-73 is still one of the most agile short-range missiles in the world. The R-74 is a modified version with a wider seeker angle (about 60 degrees) and an improved seeker head. A guided weapon designated RVV-MD is also a development of the R-73 and also has a wider seeker angle of 60 degrees and either an infrared or radar seeker head. It is claimed to have a high resistance to electronic and optical countermeasures.

During various exercises with other air forces (especially NATO partners), operating this weapon, the MiG-29 in combination with the helmet-mounted sight has demonstrated absolute superiority against other types. The R-73 is a fire-and-forget weapon, meaning that after launch the missile guides itself to the target.

R-73 thrust
vectoring
control
surfaces.

R-77 AA-12 RVV-AE

Work on the R-77 began in 1982, and it was conceived as a response to the American AIM-120 AMRAAM. The R-77 is a medium-range missile with an active radar seeker head and is thus also a fire-and-forget weapon. After it is launched it can also receive corrective commands from the firing platform and be switched to another target, switching on its own active radar for final guidance. One very interesting feature is its grid tail fins, which were also found on the Soviet SS-20 medium range ballistic missile and are now used by the Iskander tactical ballistic missile. Combined with a thrust vectoring nozzle, these surfaces give the R-77 great agility, enabling it to engage targets pulling up to 12 g. A laser proximity fuse detonates the missile's warhead. The R-77 is capable of engaging targets at heights from sixty-five feet to 82,000 feet at maximum speed of 2,200 miles per hour. It is claimed that the R-77 has been in use by the Russian military since the early 1990s, however this appears doubtful, for since then no photos showing Russian combat aircraft armed with the R-77 have appeared in the media. The R-77 has also not been seen on Russian combat aircraft operating in Syria and instead they remain armed with the R-27. The RVV-SD is a new missile with an increased range of sixty-five miles and is the successor to the R-77.

R-27 AA-10 Alamo

Like the R-73, the R-27 family of missiles was also designed for the new generation of Soviet fighter aircraft. It was designed as a medium-range missile and uses semi-active or active radar homing and IR seeker heads. The Alamo was later fitted with a larger rocket motor for greater range. It can engage targets at heights from sixty-five feet to 88,500 feet with a maximum speed of 2,175 miles per hour. The aircraft firing the missile can successfully launch while pulling up to 5 g. The semi-active variants of the R-27 should largely have been replaced by the R-27AE, however it is a considerable disadvantage to have to illuminate the target until impact, as this severely limits the maneuverability of the attacking fighter. But the introduction of the R-27AE was cancelled in favor of the R-77. If the R-27R (or R-27ER) is electronically jammed on its way to the target, it automatically guides to the jammer in order to put it out of action. The letter E in the missile's designation stands for Extended, a reference to a larger rocket motor.

Live R-27R AAMs during live firing by German Air Force MiG-29s at Eglin in 2003. *Stefan Gawlista*

GSh-301

The MiG-29 was originally to have used the AO-17A cannon. This was a twin-barreled version of the GSh-23 with a larger caliber of 30 mm. The weapon weighed 220 pounds and had a rate of fire of 3,000 rounds per minute and a muzzle velocity of 2,788 feet per second. Ultimately designated the GSh-30, this cannon was later installed in the Su-25 and Mi-24. In the Mikoyan house it was thought that at 220 pounds the GSh-30 was too heavy for the MiG-29. The first prototype MiG-29 retained a muzzle blast panel with two openings, however the GSh-30 was not installed, instead it had a weight simulating the weight of the cannon taking its place. A twin-barreled 30 mm naval cannon was modified with a single barrel that was shortened by twenty inches. The result was the GSh-301. It can be used against air and ground targets, and effective range against air targets is 656 to 2,654 feet and against ground targets 4,000 to 6,000 feet. Maximum rate of fire is from 1,500 to 1,800 rounds per minute, muzzle velocity is 2,900 feet per second. Each shell weighs approximately thirty ounces, the projectile itself about fourteen ounces. The cannon is water vapor cooled and is coupled with the aircraft's laser range finder for accuracy. The entire cannon weighs approximately 110 pounds.

Ammunition capacity of just 150 rounds was initially thought to be too little, however the cannon is only conceived as a backup weapon for close combat. As well, the caliber of the Russian cannon is greater than that of most western weapons. The projectile itself has much greater kinetic energy, and damage to the target is thus also much greater. Russian rounds also carry a larger propellant charge. Firing tests have shown that just five to seven shells are necessary to destroy an enemy fighter.

The ammunition is belted and stowed in a magazine box. The light and simple design of the GSh-301 has a disadvantage when it comes to service life, however. The barrel has to be replaced after 1,000 rounds, and the entire cannon must be serviced after 2,000 rounds. Because of the cannon's accuracy, training on the cannon is very brief, thus minimizing wear. To protect the airframe against the powerful muzzle blast, a heat-resistant steel section is added, which also absorbs some of the enormous recoil forces.

Interestingly, the cannon cannot be used with an external fuel tank suspended beneath the fuselage, as the shell casings, which are ejected between the air intakes, would damage the tank. The ejector is roughly abeam the nosewheel leg and the resulting damage could have

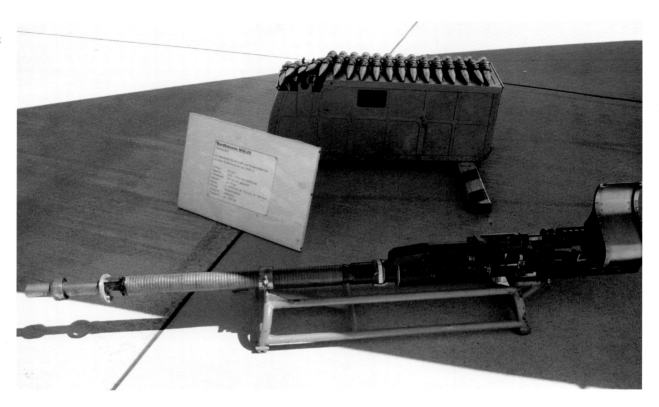

GSh-301 with
ammunition box
and belted
ammunition.

Installed
GSh-301 (seen
from below) in
the port wing
root extension.
Stefan Gawlista

catastrophic consequences. If the pilot needs to use the cannon in such a configuration he must first jettison the fuel tank. Such a situation is, however, rather improbable, for before the cannon is used as a quasi last resort the missiles would have to have been used and the external fuel tank, as the first to be emptied, would probably have been jettisoned prior to engaging in close-in combat. The cannon and ammunition box are housed in the port wing root extension.

Kh-29 AS-14 Kedge

The Kh-29 is designed for use against hardened or armored ground targets and for use against vessels. Three different seeker heads are available:

- semi-active laser guidance
- semi-active television guidance
- passive IR guidance

Use of the semi-active laser guidance required the target to be illuminated by the launching or accompanying aircraft or by personnel on the ground. The missile's seeker head receives the reflected laser beam and follows it to the target. A condition of use is that no cloud or fog be present to absorb the laser beam. When TV control is used, the rocket must be guided to the target by the weapons operator/navigator, during which deviations of six to ten feet are not exceeded. An alternate method is for the weapons operator to mark the target on the TV picture on the display, after which the seeker head guides the weapon to the target using contrast recognition. During the autonomous part of the missile's flight the pilot or weapons operator can manually transmit corrective data to the weapon. This weapon played an important role in attacking high-priority ground targets in the Soviet wars in Afghanistan and Chechnya.

Kh-31 AS-17 Krypton

The Kh-31 was developed to attack shipping (Kh-31A) and air defense radars (Kh-31P). The basic design of both versions is identical up to the warhead and seeker head. The Kh-31 had a solid-fuel booster, which accelerates the missile to the ignition speed of the ramjet engine. The Kh-31 flies to the target at its very high speed of 2,900 miles per hour, making it difficult to combat.

The Kh-31A anti-shipping version is capable of destroying ships with displacements up to 4,960 tons. It has an active radar seeker head and is a fire-and-forget weapon. The Kh-31P anti-radar version is designed to neutralize air defense, air traffic control, and early warning radars and is said to be very effective against the Patriot missile system. It has a passive radar seeker, which receives signals from the enemy radar and then guides toward the transmitter.

TV-guided Kh-29T cruise missile. In the background is the Kh-35 guided anti-shipping missile.

It is thus also a fire-and-forget weapon. The missile has a large frequency range in order to be able to detect as many enemy radars as possible.

Kh-35 URAN

The Kh-35 is an anti-shipping missile capable of destroying ships up to the cruiser class. This weapon was developed in the mid-1980s, and entered service in the early 1990s. It is equipped with an active radar seeker head, which in the final phase of flight automatically locks onto the target, making it a fire-and-forget weapon. The missile previously received target data from the launch platform and steered toward the target using its own inertial navigation system. The Kh-35's radar seeker head begins locking on at about twelve miles from the target and from there to the target is self-guided. Depending on wave height, the missile flies at a height of ten to fifty feet. The Kh-35 then flies at a speed of about 680 miles per hour. The Kh-35 can also be launched from ships and land using a solid-fuel booster to launch the missile and bring the turbofan engine to ignition speed.

The improved Kh-35UE has twice the range of the Kh-35; its radar seeker head has an acquisition range of up to thirty miles and in addition to active radar guidance incorporates passive radar and satellite guidance.

Kh-38

The Kh-38 is a new family of medium-range missiles for use at ranges of up to twenty-five miles and can be seen as the follow-up to the Kh-25. The missile travels at twice the speed of sound and can be fitted with active and passive radar seeker heads. There are also variants with satellite, laser, and infrared guidance.

Kh-58 UshKE (TP) (AS-11 Kilter)

The Kh-58 was born in the late 1970s and was originally conceived as a weapon for use by the MiG-25BM. Over the years a variety of variants of the Kh-58 were developed. One is an anti-radar missile for striking enemy

ground radars (stationary and mobile). It has a passive radar seeker head, which has a broad spectrum of different known radar sources. For radars operating in pulse mode, it covers the range between 1.2 and 11 GHz, in continuous transmit mode, the A band. The seeker head thus transmits no detectable radar impulses, instead it receives them and automatically guides toward the radar source.

Air defense radars detect the approaching missile, but the Kh-58 is flying at such a high speed during its final phase of flight (2,485 mph) and can have a reduced radar signature (radar absorbing finish), making the task of the radar under attack much more difficult. If the Kh-58 is detected in time, the target radar will turn itself off and change its position. This is partially countered by an automatically activated active radar, but not on the Kh-58UshKE (TP). This is currently the most modern version and it has additional heat sensors to enable enemy radars to be destroyed even if turned off. To enable the weapon to be used by the Sukhoi T-50, the tail fins are foldable to allow it to fit in the weapons bays. An external receiver pod is carried externally for the Kh-31 and the Kh-58 (and versions), which detects the enemy radar transmissions. The Kh-58 UshKE has smaller dimensions that precede variants and are thus more difficult to detect.

3M-14AE, 3M-54AE1, and Kh-59MK

The 3M-14AE, 3M-54AE1, and Kh-59MK/MK2/M2E are only offered for the MiG-35. The first two weapons are designs by the Novator Design Bureau in Yekaterinburg. The original versions were developed for use by Soviet submarines and surface vessels, and these in turn had their origins in the Kh-55 long-range cruise missile. The 3M-14AE is designed for use against land targets. It is stowed in a canister that is slung under the inner wing. When the weapon is fired, the actual cruise missile is ejected from the container and its engine ignited. As it is intended for use against land targets and key targets are stationary and their positions known (for example bridges, command posts, supply installations, etc.), the target's coordinates are entered into the weapon. Actual lock-on to the target by the missile's own radar takes place at about twelve miles. Operating altitude over land is 150 to 450 feet and over sea sixty feet.

The 3M-54AE1 variant is designed for use against surface vessels. It is also carried in a canister and is launched

In the middle is the Kh-31 anti-radar and anti-shipping missile.

Kh-35 anti-shipping cruise missile with folded control surfaces.

3M-14AE cruise missile.

Kh-59MK cruise missile. The grey cylinder beneath the missile body is the turbofan engine.

the same way as the 14AE. However, as ships are moving targets, the cruise missile's radar needs a significantly greater range to detect the target in time and pursue it, in this case forty miles. The somewhat smaller warhead is due to the larger radar.

The Kh-59 is a versatile guided weapon that can be equipped with a variety of seeker heads. The Kh-59MK is designed for use against shipping. It flies at a height of about thirty to forty-five feet and during its final approach to the target descends to as low as twelve feet, to make enemy countermeasures more difficult. The Kh-59MK2 is intended for use against land targets. It flies at heights between 150 and 900 feet. It can also be programmed with

the location of a stationary target. During the final approach to the target, an active radar provides final guidance. Propulsion is provided by a turbofan engine located beneath the missile. Because of the size and weight of these three missiles, they can only be carried on the innermost stores racks.

In keeping with an arms agreement between Russia and the USA, the range of exported air-to-ground cruise missiles is limited to 180 miles.

Guided Bombs

The first of these are the KAB-500L and KAB-1500L laser-guided bombs, weighing 1,100 and 3,300 pounds respectively. With laser guidance it is necessary to illuminate the target until it is struck by the bomb. This can be done with a special targeting pod on the aircraft itself or by an accompanying aircraft. It is also possible for troops on the ground to mark the target with a portable laser target designator. This is only possible in clear weather, however, for the laser beam is absorbed by clouds or heavy fog.

The KAB-500Kr and KAB-1500Kr are TV-guided bombs weighing 1,100 and 3,300 pounds respectively. They are equipped with a TV camera in the nose and transmit a television picture to the cockpit of the aircraft. There the pilot or weapons control officer marks the target on the display. The seeker head keeps the target in the crosshairs, including by contrast recognition, and the bomb steers itself to the target using movable control surfaces. Here too good weather conditions are required. Laser- and TV-guided bombs can be used against a variety of targets including bunkers, bridges, key targets, and pinpoint targets requiring a high degree of accuracy.

A guided bomb was required for the Sukhoi T-50 that enabled a suitable number of weapons to be carried in its weapons bay. A 550-pound guided bomb was chosen and it can also be carried by the MiG-29. The guidance methods are identical to those described above.

The KAB-500S was developed for use in bad weather or at night. It is a GPS-controlled bomb that receives its position information from the Russian GLONASS satellite navigation system.

The Russian optics maker UOMS developed the SAPSAN-E targeting pod to enable aircraft to use guided weapons without external laser illumination. It contains a thermal imaging system plus laser range finder, target illuminator and tracker, and a receiver for illuminated targets. The thermal imaging system also makes it possible to use other guided weapons in conditions of poor visibility. The pod weighs 550 pounds.

Grom

The Grom guided weapon has so far been offered in two variants, a guided missile (Grom-E1) and a glide bomb (Grom-E2). This guided weapon is based on the Kh-38, which is also new. It is a standoff weapon, about which no range figures or flight parameters have been revealed. Guidance is provided by a combined inertial navigation and satellite receiver system.

Unguided Weapons

In addition to the guided weapons just described, the MiG-29 can carry a variety of unguided munitions, including large-caliber rockets and a considerable range of freefall bombs. The MiG-29 can also carry bomb dispensers.

KAB-500Kr
TV-guided
bomb.

KAB-500L
laser-guided
bomb.

Free-fall bombs
and cluster
bomb
containers.

SAPSAN-E
targeting pod.

Guided Weapons				
Designation	Weight (lb)	Weight of explosive (lb)	Range/Target Deviation	Guidance
R-73	231	16.5	18.5 mi	infrared
R-77	385	50	48 mi	active radar
R-77SD	418	66	66 mi	active radar
R-27T	540	86	30–42 mi	infrared
R-27TE	782	86	42–60 mi	infrared
R-27R	557	86	30–42 mi	semi-active radar
R-27RE	782	86	42–60 mi	semi-active radar
R-27AE	767	86	42–60 mi	active radar
Kh-29TE	1,521	705	12–18 mi	TV
Kh-29L	1,455	705	4.5–6 mi	laser
Kh-31A	1,344	207	42 mi	active radar
Kh-31AD	1,576	242	72–96 mi	active radar
Kh-31P	1,322	192	67 mi	passive radar
Kh-31PD	1,576	242	67–155 mi	passive radar
Kh-35U	1,146	320	78 mi	active radar
Kh-35UE	1,212	320	156 mi	active radar, GPS
Kh-38	1,146	max. 551	25 mi	laser, radar, IR, GPS
Kh-59MK	2,050	705	177 mi	active radar
3M-14AE	3,086	992	360 mi	active radar
3M-54AE1	4,300	880	360 mi	active radar
KAB-500L	1,100	430	12–21 ft	laser
KAB-1500L	3,307	463–1,433	12–21 ft	laser
KAB-500Kr	1,146	220–308	12–21 ft	TV
KAB-1500Kr	3,362	970	12–21 ft	TV
KAB-500S	1,235	430	21–36 ft	satellite
Grom-E1	1,235	551	unknown	–
Grom-E2	1,235	551 + 287 (2 warheads)	unknown	–
SAPSAN-E[2]	551	–	–	FLIR, TV, laser
Litening[2]	456	–	–	FLIR, TV, laser
Damocles[2]	584	–	–	FLIR, TV, laser

Appendices

Appendix A: Specifications

MiG-29 Specification							
	MiG-29	MiG-29UB	MiG-29	MiG-29S	MiG-29SD	MiG-29SE	MiG-29SM
OKB Designation	9.12	9.51	9.13	9.13S	9.12SD	9.13SE	9.13SM
Overall length (ft)	56.8	57.1	56.8	56.8	56.8	56.8	56.8
Wingspan (ft)	37.3	37.3	37.3	37.3	37.3	37.3	37.3
Wing area (ft²)	409	409	409	409	409	409	409
Height (ft)	15.5	15.5	15.5	15.5	15.5	15.5	15.5
Max. takeoff weight (lb)	40,785	41,667	41,447	43,431	40,785	43,431	44,092
Weapons load (lb)	5,070	5,070	7,055	8,818	8,818	9,920	8,818
Internal fuel weight (lb)	7,055	7,055	7,500	7,500	7,055	7,500	7,500
Fuel weight with external tanks (lb)	9,700[1]	9,700[1]	13,668[2]	14,110[2]	13,668[2]	14,110[2]	14,110[2]
Power plants	RD-33 Series II	RD-33 Series II	RD-33 Series II	RD-33 Series II	RD-33 Series II	RD-33 Series II	RD-33 Series II
Maximum dry thrust (lb)	11,015	11,015	11,015	11,015	11,015	11,015	11,015
Maximum afterburner (lb)	18,210	18,210	18,210	18,210	18,210	18,210	18,210
Maximum speed at ground level (mph)	932	870	932	932	932	932	932
Maximum speed at 32,800 ft. (mph)	1,522	1,385	1,522	1,522	1,522	1,522	1,522
Range on internal fuel (mi) 932	870	994	994	932	994	994	
Range with external tanks (mi)	1,305[2]	1,243[1]	1,802[2]	1,740[2]	1,802[2]	1,802[2]	1,802[2]
Service ceiling (ft)	57,415	57,415	55,774	55,774	57,415	55,774	55,774
Maximum climb (ft/min)	64,960	64,960	59,055	59,055	64,960	59,055	59,055
Maximum g load	9 g	9 g	9 g	9 g	9 g	9 g	9 g
First flight	1977	1981	1984	1990	1995	1992	1995

[1] With 396 gallon tank (2,645 lb) external fuselage tank
[2] With fuselage tank and either two 396 gallon (2,645 lb) or two 304 gallon
(1,896 lb) underwing tanks

MiG-29 Radar Specifications

Type	N-019	N-019M	N-010	N-010ME	N-010AE	BARS-29
Range (radar reflective area: 32.3 ft²) mi	50	56	62	75	100	75
Maximum number of tracked targets	10	10	10	10	30	15
Number of targets capable of being attacked simultaneously	1	2	4	4	8	4
Installed in	MiG-29	MiG-29S	MiG-29M (9.12) MiG-29K	MiG-29SMT K (9.41)	MiG-35	MiG-29OVT
Creation of ground maps	–	–	x	x	x	x
Weight (lb)	771	838	551	485	507	551

MiG-29 Specification

	MiG-29M	MiG-29K	MiG-29SMT-II	MiG-29SMT	MiG-29UBT	MiG-29KUB	MiG-29M1-M2
OKB Designation	9.15	9.31	9.17-II	9.19	9.52	9.41/9.47	9.61/9.67
Overall length (ft)	56.8	56.7	56.8	56.8	57	56.75	56.75
Wingspan (ft)	37.3	39*	37.2	37.2	37.2	39*	39
Wing area (ft²)	409	463	409	409	409	452	409
Height (ft)	15.5	15.5	15.5	15.5	15.5	14.4	15.4
Max. takeoff weight (lb)	48,501	49,384	45.195	48,501	46,297	54,013	49,384 (M1) 52,250 (M2)
Weapons load (lb)	9,920	9,920	8,818	9,920	9,920	12,125	14,330
Internal fuel weight (lb)	9,920	9,920	10,582	8,818	10,582	11,685** 10,582	11,685** 10,582
Fuel weight with external tanks (lb)	16,535²	16,535²	16,975²	15,432	16,975	23,590*** 22,487***	23,590*** 22,487***
Power plants	RD-33K	RD-33K³	RD-33 Series 3	RD-33 Series 3	RD-33 Series 3	RD-33MK	RD-33MK
Maximum dry thrust (lb)	11,915	11,915	11,915	11,015	11,015	11,690	11,690
Maximum afterburner (lb)	19,333	20,682³	19,333	18,210	18,210	19,783	19,333
Maximum speed at ground level (mph)	932	870	932	932	870	870	932
Maximum speed at 32,800 ft. (mph)	1,553	1,429	1,522	1,491	1,385	1,305	1,522
Range on internal fuel (mi)	1,243	1,118	1,367	1,118	1,305	1,553*** 1,056	1,553*** 1,056
Range with external tanks (mi)	1,988	1,864	2,050	1,864	1,926	1,864*** 1,678	1,864*** 1,678
Service ceiling (ft)	55,774	57,087	55,774	57,415	57,415	57,415	57,415
Maximum Climb (ft/min)	62,992	51,181	59,055				
Maximum g load 9g	8.5g	9g	9g	9g	8g	9g	
First flight	1986	1988	2000	2005	1998	2006	2001

³ The MiG-29K was powered by a naval version of the RD-33K, the only difference being an additional brief increase in power which could be used at high-gross takeoffs. The engine was also adapted to endure the difficult conditions at sea.
* Wingspan with wings folded is 25.6 feet.
** Data for the MiG-29M1/K (MiG-35/33), less * data for MiG-29M2/KUB (MiG-35D, MiG-33D)
*** With four 304-gallon external wing tanks and a larger 568-gallon fuselage centerline tank

Appendix B: MiG-29K 9.41 Cutaway Drawing
(Alexey Micheyev)

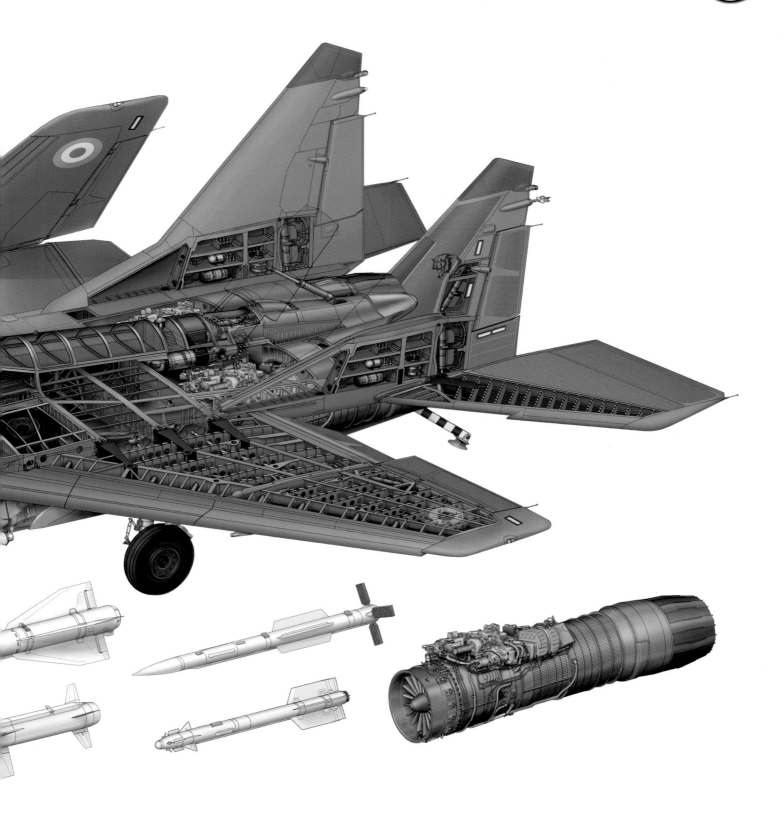

Appendix C: Cockpit

Forward cockpit with ejection seat removed.

Appendix D: Camouflage Schemes
(Mariusz Wojciechowski)

968th Fighter
Regiment of the
16th Air Army
(Altenburg, East
Germany)

Aircraft of a
Guards
Regiment

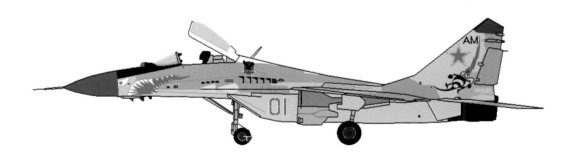

1521st Center
for Combat
Training (Mary,
Turkmen SSR
1991)

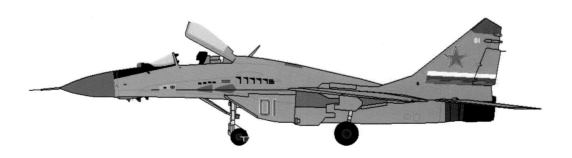

426th Aviation
Squadron
(Russian base at
Jerewan,
Armenia 2007)

14th Fighter
Regiment, Kursk,
Russia

Algeria

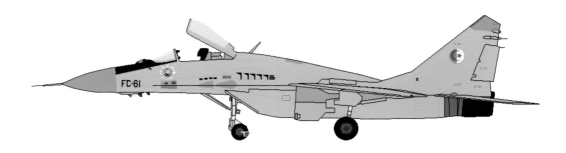

Azerbaijan

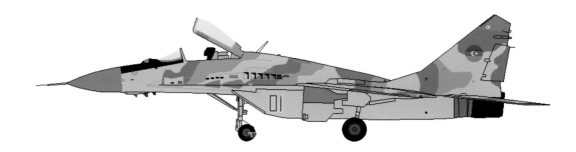

Bangladesh

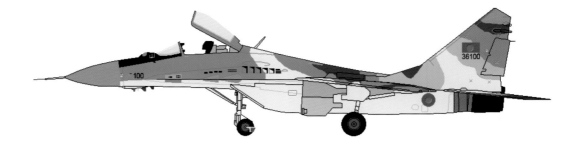

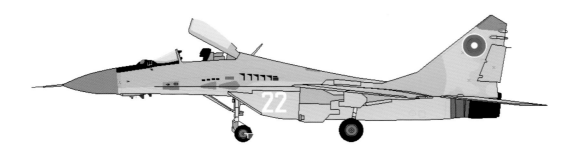

Bulgaria

JG 3 Vladimir Komarov at Preschen, East Germany

Two-seater JG 3 Vladimir Komarov at Preschen, East Germany

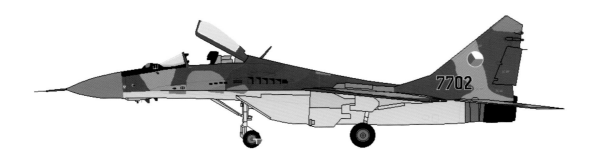

Czechoslovakia

1st Fighter
Squadron at Siliac,
Slovakia

1st Fighter
Squadron at Siliac,
Slovakia, digital
camouflage Eritrea

India

India

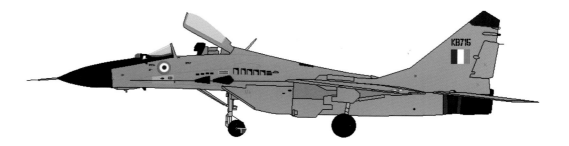

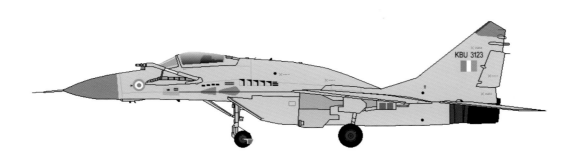

India

Iraq

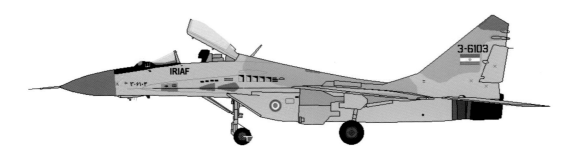

Iran

Yemen

Yugoslavia

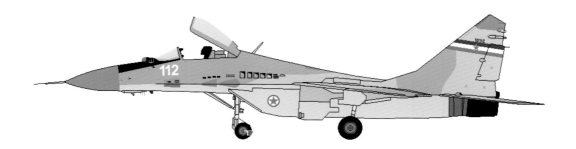

Serbia

Kazakhstan

Cuba

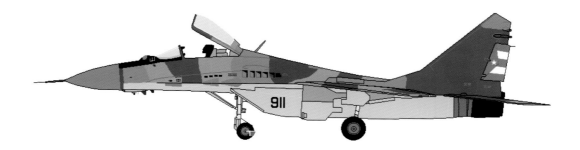

Cuba

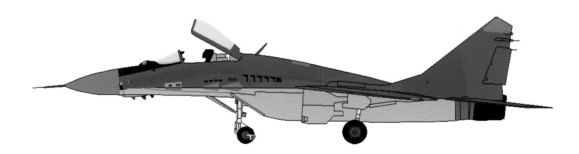

Moldavia

Myanmar
(formerly Burma)

North Korea

Peru

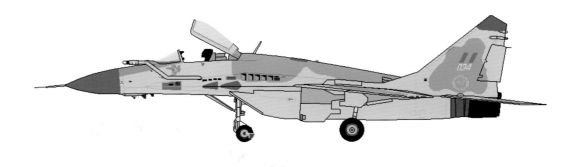

Poland

Romania

Sudan

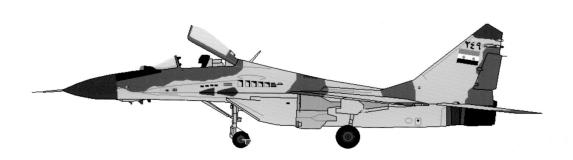

Syria

Ukraine

Ukraine

Hungary

16th Naval Air Station
Fallon, Nevada (USA)

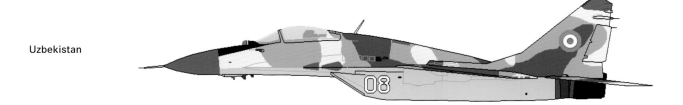

Uzbekistan

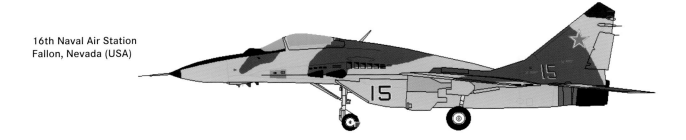

White Russia

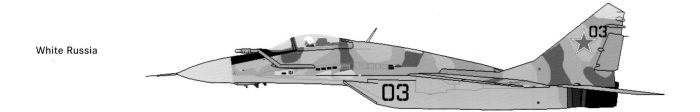

Appendix E: Test Pilots

Alexander Vasilievich Fedotov
06/23/1932 – 04/04/1984

Test pilot with the MiG OKB from 1958–84. Conducted the MiG-29's maiden flight in 1977. Fedotov was killed during the flight test of a MiG-31.

Anatoly Nikolayevich Kvochur
Born 04/16/1952

Test pilot with the MiG OKB from 1981–91. Tested the MiG-29K, representative of the LII GROMOV Flight Research Institute and played an important role in the development of Russian cockpit displays.

Valery Evgenyeva Menitsky
02/08/1944 – 01/18/2008

Test pilot with the MiG OKB from 1969–92. Tested the MiG-29 prototypes and the MiG-29M. Chief test pilot with MiG, CEO of the airline ATLANT-SOYUZ.

Roman Petrovich Taskaev
Born 10/14/1954

Test pilot with the MiG OKB from 1983–98. Tested the MiG-29K, set world altitude record of 90,091 feet with the MiG-29 on 04/26/1995. Since 1998 he has been a test pilot with the Yakovlev OKB.

Aviard Gavrilovich Fastovets
07/05/1937 – 09/05/1991

Test pilot with the MiG OKB from 1967–87. Conducted the first flight in the MiG-29UB in 1981. Carried out tests of the T-1 and T-2 ski jumps in the MiG-29 from 1982–84. Fastovets was killed in the crash of a MiG-31 in 1991.

Boris Antonovich Orlov
Born 01/09/1934

Test pilot with the MiG OKB from 1965–87. Test flew MiG-29 prototypes, subsequently became leading engineer in the MiG OKB.

Toktar Ongarbaevich Aubakirov
Born 07/27/1946

Test pilot with the MiG OKB from 1976–92, test flew the MiG-29K, first deck landing and launch in a MiG-29K from the carrier *Tbilisi* in 1989. In 1991, he served as a MIR cosmonaut, from 1993–96 he was director of the Kazakh Air and Spaceflight Agency, and subsequently held several state offices.

Alexander Yuryevich Garnaev
Born 09/01/1960

Test pilot with the MiG OKB from 1987–94. Test flew the MiG-29M, for many years was a test pilot with the GROMOV Flight Research Institute.

All photos: RAC MiG

Marat Raviliyevich Alykov
Born 08/20/1959

Test pilot with the MiG OKB since 1987.
Test flew the MiG-29SM, SMT, UBT, and
MiG-29M2.

Mikhail Belyayev

Chief test pilot with the MiG OKB.

Vladimir Mikhailovich Gorbunov
Born 06/14/1946

Test pilot at the GROMOV Flight Research
Institute from 1982–91. Test pilot with
the MiG OKB from 1991, test flew the
MiG-29SMT.

Stanislav Gorbunov

Project pilot on the MiG-35 and MiG-29K.

Pavel Nikolayevich Vlasov
Born 10/13/1960

Test pilot with the MiG OKB since 1989,
from 2002, chief test pilot and deputy
general director with MiG. First flight
and testing of the MiG-29OVT, test flew
the MiG-33 and MiG-35.

All photos: RAC MiG

Bibliography

Literature

Gordon, Yefim, *Mikoyan MiG-29 Fulcrum*, MBI Publishing Company 1999.

Gordon, Yefim, Fomin Andrej, Michejev Alexej, *MiG-29*, OAO Ljubimaja Kniga 1998.

Gordon, Yefim, Alan Dawes, *Russian Airpower*, Airlife Publishing Ltd. 2002.

Kopenhagen, Wilfried, *Waffenarsenal Band 141*, Podzun Pallas Verlag 1993.

Markowski, Viktor, *Heißer Himmel über Afghanistan*, Elbe Dnepr Verlag, 2006.

Tonk, Stefan, *Triebwerkschronik JG-73 "Steinhoff,"* 2004.

Air Fleet, 3/2000

Airforce Monthly, 2009; 9/2014

Flieger-Revue, 2/89; 3/89; 2/96; 10/2000; 11/2000; 6/2003; 7/2006; 9/2008

Flieger-Revue Extra, 6; 20; 21; 22

Flug-Revue, 9/95 10/98; 11/2001; 4/2006

Take-Off Magazine, 5/2006; 5/2008

Russia & CIS Observer, 5/2006

Internet

aces.safarikovi.org

acig.info/CMS/

airvectors.net

defenseindustrydaily.com

eng.ktrv.ru

www.fabulousfulcrums.de

flightglobal.com

g-friedens-forschung.de

globalsecurity.org

www.mars.slupsk.pl/fort/mig/default.htm

MIGAVIA

www.military-heat.com

Ria Novosti

ruaviation.com

sudantribune.com

www.theaviationist.com

Andy Gröning is a trained tool mechanic and worked for twelve years as a professional soldier in the Bundeswehr, including six years as an engine mechanic on the MiG-29; he was present when the aircraft was retired. His primary interest is Soviet-Russian military aviation.